**Dr Michael M. Gruneberg**, designer and writer of the Gruneberg Linkword Language Course, is widely acknowledged as an international expert on memory improvement. A Senior Lecturer in Psychology at University College, Swansea, he has published a large number of articles in scientific journals, as well as a number of well-known books on the application of memory research. He has also lectured widely in both the UK and the USA and addressed several international scientific conferences. In 1988 he provided the original script for and appeared in *The Magic of Memory*, a programme in the BBC television QED series which illustrated many memory techniques, including his own Linkword Method.

The Linkword Courses have grown out of a large body of published scientific research showing that the imagery method they employ is highly effective in improving the memory for foreign language vocabulary. One study has shown that using this method increases retention from 28% to 88% for a list of 60 Spanish words. Dr Gruneberg has taken this work considerably further, working with linguists and setting out images and testing patterns to create a fully-integrated language-learning system capable of teaching both vocabulary and grammar.

Since it was first published in 1987, the Linkword system has been both highly successful and widely acclaimed.

*LANGUAGE CONSULTANT*
**Gabriel C. Jacobs B.A., Ph.D.**, Lecturer in French Studies, University College of Swansea, Wales. Dr Jacobs has been involved for many years in the practical application of language teaching.

D1343782

'We have found the Linkword programmes to be both effective and entertaining'
*Brian Ablett, Training Development Officer, formerly with British Caledonian*

'Feel free to quote me as a satisfied customer'
*Michael Woodhall, formerly Director Language Learning Centre, Manchester Business School*

'It took 12 hours to teach a regime that normally takes 40 hours'
*Peter Marsh, Thomson Holidays*

'I was frankly astounded at how effective this visual imagery was as an aid to memory retention'
*Lolita Taylor, Popular Computer World*

'I tried the system out in both German and French and was amazed at how quickly it worked'
*Jan McCann, Toronto Sun*

'I learned German vocabulary at about twice the speed . . . If you want to learn or brush up on a foreign language, this system will accelerate your learning beyond anything you have experienced in conventional foreign-language instruction'
*Professor Douglas J. Herrman, Applied Cognitive Psychology*

## Also by Dr Michael Gruneberg

LINKWORD LANGUAGE SYSTEM: FRENCH
LINKWORD LANGUAGE SYSTEM: GERMAN
LINKWORD LANGUAGE SYSTEM: SPANISH
LINKWORD LANGUAGE SYSTEM: ITALIAN
LINKWORD LANGUAGE SYSTEM: GREEK
LINKWORD LANGUAGE SYSTEM: PORTUGUESE

and published by Corgi Books

# LINKWORD
# LANGUAGE SYSTEM

# FURTHER FRENCH

## Dr Michael M. Gruneberg

*Language Consultant*
**Gabriel C. Jacobs BA PhD**

**CORGI BOOKS**

# LINKWORD: FURTHER FRENCH

## A CORGI BOOK 0 552 13916 5

First publication in Great Britain

PRINTING HISTORY
Corgi edition published 1992

Copyright © Dr Michael Gruneberg 1985

This book is set in 9/10pt Century
by Colset Private Limited, Singapore.

Corgi Books are published by Transworld Publishers Ltd., 61–63 Uxbridge Road, Ealing, London W5 5SA, in Australia by Transworld Publishers (Australia) Pty. Ltd., 15–23 Helles Avenue, Moorebank, NSW 2170, and in New Zealand by Transworld Publishers (N.Z.) Ltd., 3 William Pickering Drive, Albany, Auckland.

Printed and bound in Great Britain by
Cox & Wyman Ltd., Reading, Berks.

# *Contents*

# TEST YOURSELF WITH LINKWORD

Picture each of these images in your mind's eye for about ten seconds. For example, the French for *tablecloth* is *nappe*. Imagine yourself having a nap on a tablecloth, as vividly as you can, for about ten seconds.

○ The French for TABLECLOTH is NAPPE
Imagine having a *NAP* on a *TABLECLOTH*.

○ The German for GENTLEMEN is HERREN
Imagine a *HERRING* dangling from the door of a *GENTLEMEN'S* toilet.

○ The Italian for FLY is MOSCA.
Imagine *FLIES* invading *MOSCOW*.

○ The Spanish for SUITCASE is MALETA
Imagine *MY LETTER* in your *SUITCASE*.

○ The French for HEDGEHOG is HERISSON.
Imagine your *HAIRY SON* looks like a *HEDGEHOG*.

○ The German for LETTER is BRIEF.
Imagine a *BRIEF LETTER*.

○ The Italian for DRAWER is CASSETTO.
Imagine you keep *CASSETTES* in a *DRAWER*.

○ The Spanish for WAITRESS is CAMARERA.
Imagine a *WAITRESS* with a *CAMERA* slung around her neck!

## NOW TURN OVER

○ What is the English for CAMARERA? _____

○ What is the English for CASSETTO? _____

○ What is the English for BRIEF? _____

○ What is the English for HERISSON? _____

○ What is the English for MALETA? _____

○ What is the English for MOSCA? _____

○ What is the English for HERREN? _____

○ What is the English for NAPPE? _____

## TURN BACK FOR THE ANSWERS

Do not expect to get them all correct at the first attempt. However, if you feel you got more right than you normally would have – then this course will suit you!

# WHO IS *FURTHER LINKWORD FRENCH* FOR?

- For holidaymakers
- For business
- For school work

This book is designed for *anyone* with a basic knowledge of French – *whether or not* they have used *Linkword French\** – who wants a fast, easy way of boosting his or her vocabulary and grammar to the point where everyday communication is possible. If you have not used Linkword before, Section 12 on Page 261 gives the vocabulary and grammar covered in *Linkword French* so that you can assess easily whether or not you have reached the standard needed to use the present book. Obviously if you have any difficulty with Section 12, you should start with *Linkword French*.

The Linkword Courses have been carefully designed to teach you an extensive vocabulary and a basic grammar in a simple step-by-step way that anyone can follow. After about 10–12 hours, or even less, you will have a vocabulary of literally hundreds of words and the ability to string these further words together to form sentences that can be used to communicate in a large number of everyday situations. The course is ideal, therefore, for the holidaymaker or business person who just wants the basics in a hurry so that he or she can be understood, e.g. in the hotel, arriving at the destination, sightseeing, eating out, in emergencies, telling the time and so on.

The course is also an ideal supplement to schoolwork. Many school pupils feel that they remember words for the first time when introduced to the Linkword system, and understand basic grammar for the first time too!

Finally this book is ideal for those who have learned French at school some time ago but who are now rusty. Linkword is an ideal revision course, covering much of the vocabulary and grammar you learned (or should have learned!) at school in a quick and painless way, so that it will all come flooding back.

**Note**
*Linkword French* is the first basic Linkword French book. For future reference it will be described as Linkword I.

# HOW TO USE LINKWORD

1] You will be presented with words like this:
The French for TABLECLOTH is NAPPE
Imagine having a NAP on a TABLECLOTH
What you do is to imagine this picture in your mind's eye as vividly as possible.

2] After you have read the image you should think about it in your mind's eye for about 10 seconds before moving on to the next word. If you do not spend enough time thinking about the image it will not stick in your memory as well as it should.

3] Sometimes the word in French and in English is the same or very similar. For example, the French for 'taxi' is 'taxi'. When this happens you will be asked to associate the word in some way with the Eiffel Tower.

Imagine a taxi driving under the Eiffel Tower. Whenever the Eiffel Tower comes to mind, therefore, you will know the word is the same or similar in both English and French.

4] The sentence examples given in the course may well strike you as silly and bizarre. They have deliberately been given in this way to show up points of grammar and to get away from the idea that you should remember useful phrases 'parrot fashion'. However, during the course, some 'sensible' sentence examples are given to show you how easy it is to use your knowledge in real life, everyday situations.

5] **PRONUNCIATION**
This course is designed for learners who already have a knowledge of French pronunciation. The exact pronunciation of each word is, however, given on the audio tape which accompanies this course and which is available from Corgi books.

# SOME USEFUL HINTS

1. You should start by making sure that you are familiar with the words and grammar given in Section 12 of the book (p. 261). If you find that you are having difficulty with this or that you are not familiar with either the vocabulary or the grammar, you should start by reading the First Linkword French book.

2. Take a break of about 10 minutes between each section, and always stop if you feel tired.

3. Don't worry about forgetting a few words, and do not go back to relearn words you have forgotten. Just think of how much you are learning, and try to pick up the forgotten words when it comes to revising.

4. Revise after Section 4, Section 8 and at the end of the course. Then revise the whole course a week later and a month later.

5. Don't worry if you forget some of the words or grammar after a time. Relearning is extremely fast, and going through the book for a few hours just before you go abroad will quickly get you back to where you were.

6. The course will not give you conversational fluency. You can't expect this until you go abroad and live in a country for a period of time. What it will give you very rapidly is the ability to survive in a large number of situations you will meet abroad. It will also give you a substantial enough vocabulary and grammar to provide a platform from which you can become fluent and give you a really sound basic grounding for school work.

# IMPORTANT NOTES

1. Linkword is probably unique among language courses in teaching not only *what* to learn, but *how* to remember what you have learned. The major principle used to teach you how to remember is the keyword or Linkword technique which has been shown in a number of scientific studies to improve memory for vocabulary substantially. For this reason Linkword courses emphasise the importance of learning a large vocabulary just as much as basic grammar. Indeed, it can be argued that if you know the relevant words in French but not the grammar, you might well be understood. If you know the grammar but not the words, communication is impossible! Of course, grammar is important in helping you to communicate, and this course, *together with* the basic grammar of Linkword I (see Section 12, p. 261) covers the use of articles, genders, plurals, personal and possessive pronouns, agreements, present, past and future tense, negatives, formation of questions, conjunctions, prepositions and word order – enough for proper sentence construction in the everyday situations you are likely to meet abroad.

2. The 'Linkword' in the images you will be given is the word in English which helps you to remember what the French word you are trying to learn is. For example, the French for 'rice' is 'riz'. Imagine you *raise* rice. 'Raise' is the Linkword. The Linkword does not have to sound exactly like the French word i.e. riz in this example, in order to help you to remember, so long as it is similar in sound to the French word and you know how the French word is pronounced. Although this book does assume that you know how to pronounce French words, if you are in any doubt, you should play the appropriate section of the pronunciation tape which accompanies this book, before you start each section.

# Section 1   FOOD, FAMILY AND SAILING

Here are five useful food words to start with

## THINK OF EACH IMAGE IN YOUR MIND'S EYE FOR ABOUT TEN SECONDS

○ The French for RICE is RIZ
  Imagine you RAISE rice.

○ The French for CHICKEN is POULET
  Imagine a chicken hanging from a PULLEY.

○ The French for SALT is SEL
  Imagine you SELL salt.

○ The French for SAUCE is SAUCE
  Imagine you pour SAUCE from the top of the Eiffel Tower.

○ The French for SUGAR is SUCRE
  Imagine you are a SUCKER for sugar.

## YOU CAN WRITE YOUR ANSWERS IN

○ What is the English for SUCRE? _____

○ What is the English for SAUCE? _____

○ What is the English for SEL? _____

○ What is the English for POULET? _____

○ What is the English for RIZ? _____

TURN BACK FOR THE ANSWERS

## ELEMENTARY GRAMMAR

All nouns in French are either MASCULINE or FEMININE, even though they may never have been alive.

Because you cannot tell whether a word is masculline or feminine just by listening to it, you will now be shown how to remember the gender of words in French.

If the word is MASCULINE, always associate it in your mind's eye with a boxer.

For example,

RABBIT is MASCULINE in French:

Imagine a boxer punching a rabbit.

Every time you see a word with a boxer, you will know that it is masculine.

If the word is FEMININE, always imagine the word interacting with a bottle of French perfume. For example,

COW is FEMININE in French.

Imagine a cow with a bottle of perfume dangling from her neck.

When you see a bottle of perfume in your mind's eye interacting with a word, you will know the word is feminine in French.

## GENDERS

### THINK OF EACH IMAGE IN YOUR MIND'S EYE FOR ABOUT TEN SECONDS

○ The gender of RICE is MASCULINE            LE RIZ
   Imagine a boxer being showered with rice.

○ The gender of CHICKEN is MASCULINE      LE POULET
   Imagine a chicken in the ring with a boxer.

○ The gender of SALT is MASCULINE            LE SEL
   Imagine a boxer throwing salt over his left
   shoulder for luck.

○ The gender of SAUCE is FEMININE          LA SAUCE
   Imagine adding perfume to your sauce to
   flavour it.

○ The gender of SUGAR is MASCULINE       LE SUCRE
   Imagine a boxer throwing sugar over his
   shoulder instead of salt.

## YOU CAN WRITE YOUR ANSWERS IN

○ What is the gender and French for sugar? _____

○ What is the gender and French for sauce? _____

○ What is the gender and French for salt? _____

○ What is the gender and French for chicken? _____

○ What is the gender and French for rice? _____

TURN BACK FOR THE ANSWERS

Now cover up the answers below and translate the following:

(You can write your answers in)

1. THE CHICKEN IS BLACK AND WHITE
2. THE SALT IS IN THE CUPBOARD
3. I WANT THE SUGAR
4. SHE HAS THE SAUCE
5. WHERE IS THE CHICKEN?

The answers are:

1. LE POULET EST NOIR ET BLANC
2. LE SEL EST DANS L'ARMOIRE (or LE PLACARD)
3. JE VEUX LE SUCRE
4. ELLE A LA SAUCE
5. OÙ EST LE POULET?

If you find difficulty in answering these questions because you do not know the grammar or vocabulary being used, you should start with Linkword I.

# FAMILY WORDS

## THINK OF EACH IMAGE IN YOUR MIND'S EYE FOR ABOUT TEN SECONDS

○ The French for FAMILY is FAMILLE
Imagine taking your FAMILY up the Eiffel Tower.

○ The French for GRANDSON is PETIT-FILS
Imagine being charged PETTY FEES for your grandson's education.

○ The French for PEOPLE is GENS
Imagine King JOHN talking to all his people.

○ The French for UNCLE is ONCLE
Imagine taking your UNCLE to see the Eiffel Tower.

○ The French for AUNT is TANTE
Imagine thinking thaT AUNT is my aunt.

○ The French for RELATION is PARENT
Imagine your PARENTS are your closest relations.

○ The French for COUSIN (male) is COUSIN
Imagine you aCCUSE A cousin wrongly.

○ The French for COUSIN (female) is COUSINE
Imagine taking your female COUSIN up the Eiffel Tower.

○ The French for HUMAN BEING is ÊTRE HUMAIN
Imagine a cannibal ATE REMAINS of a human being.

○ The French for BRIDE is ÉPOUSE
Imagine a bride saying 'HERE PUSS' to a black cat at her wedding.

## YOU CAN WRITE YOUR ANSWERS IN

○ What is the English for ÉPOUSE? _____

○ What is the English for ÊTRE HUMAIN? _____

○ What is the English for COUSINE? _____

○ What is the English for COUSIN? _____

○ What is the English for PARENT? _____

○ What is the English for TANTE? _____

○ What is the English for ONCLE? _____

○ What is the English for GENS? _____

○ What is the English for PETIT-FILS? _____

○ What is the English for FAMILLE? _____

### TURN BACK FOR THE ANSWERS

## GENDERS

**THINK OF EACH IMAGE IN YOUR MIND'S EYE FOR ABOUT TEN SECONDS**

○ The gender of FAMILY is FEMININE
Imagine a family spraying perfume over each other.
      **LA FAMILLE**

○ The gender of GRANDSON is MASCULINE
Imagine a huge boxer punching your small grandson.
      **LE PETIT-FILS**

○ The word PEOPLE is PLURAL
      **LES GENS**

○ The gender of UNCLE is MASCULINE
Imagine your uncle in a boxing match.
      **L'ONCLE (m)**

○ The gender of AUNT is FEMININE
Imagine giving your aunt some lavender water perfume.
      **LA TANTE**

○ The gender of RELATION is MASCULINE
Imagine you set a boxer on your relation.
      **LE PARENT**

○ The gender of COUSIN (male) is MASCULINE
Imagine your male cousin in a boxing ring.
      **LE COUSIN**

○ The gender of COUSIN (female) is FEMININE
Imagine sending your female cousin a bottle of perfume.
      **LA COUSINE**

○ The gender of HUMAN BEING is MASCULINE
Imagine all human beings want to be boxers.
      **L'ÊTRE HUMAIN (m)**

○ The gender of BRIDE is FEMININE
Imagine a bride spraying herself with perfume before going to the church.
      **L'ÉPOUSE (f)**

# YOU CAN WRITE YOUR ANSWERS IN

○ What is the gender and French for bride? _____

○ What is the gender and French for
   human being? _____

○ What is the gender and French for
   cousin (female)? _____

○ What is the gender and French for
   cousin (male)? _____

○ What is the gender and French for
   relation? _____

○ What is the gender and French for aunt? _____

○ What is the gender and French for
   uncle? _____

○ What is the French for people? _____

○ What is the gender and French for
   grandson? _____

○ What is the gender and French for
   family? _____

## TURN BACK FOR THE ANSWERS

**Note**
The word PEOPLE is a plural word. The gender can vary, but think
of it as masculine.

## THE PEOPLE is LES GENS

## SOME ADJECTIVES

## THINK OF EACH IMAGE IN YOUR MIND'S EYE FOR ABOUT TEN SECONDS

○ The French for ALONE is SEUL
Imagine a poor SOUL all ALONE.

○ The French for POOR is PAUVRE
Imagine the POOR in POVERTY.

○ The French for DIFFERENT is DIFFÉRENT
Imagine the Eiffel Tower somehow looks DIFFERENT.

○ The French for WELL-BEHAVED is SAGE
Imagine giving a WELL-BEHAVED child some SAGE and onion stuffing as a reward.

○ The French for ready is PRÊT
Imagine you PRAY that your partner will get READY in time.

○ The French for POPULAR is POPULAIRE
Imagine the Eiffel Tower is a POPULAR sight.

○ The French for DARK (of hair or skin) is BRUN
Imagine wearing a DARK BROWN wig.

○ The French for SINCERE is SINCÈRE
Imagine a SINCERE CENSOR.

○ The French for ELEGANT is ÉLÉGANT
Imagine being very ELEGANT as you fall from the Eiffel Tower.

○ The French for HAPPY is HEUREUX
Imagine shouting 'HOORAY!' because you are so HAPPY.

## YOU CAN WRITE YOUR ANSWERS IN

○ What is the English for HEUREUX? _____

○ What is the English for ÉLÉGANT? _____

○ What is the English for SINCÈRE? _____

○ What is the English for BRUN? _____

○ What is the English for POPULAIRE? _____

○ What is the English for PRÊT? _____

○ What is the English for SAGE? _____

○ What is the English for DIFFÉRENT? _____

○ What is the English for PAUVRE? _____

○ What is the English for SEUL? _____

**TURN BACK FOR THE ANSWERS**

## COVER UP THE LEFT HAND PAGE

○ What is the French for happy? _____

○ What is the French for elegant? _____

○ What is the French for sincere? _____

○ What is the French for dark? _____

○ What is the French for popular? _____

○ What is the French for ready? _____

○ What is the French for well behaved? _____

○ What is the French for different? _____

○ What is the French for poor? _____

○ What is the French for alone? _____

TURN BACK FOR THE ANSWERS

**Note**

For the words you have just learned:

DIFFERENT is DIFFÉRENT (masculine), DIFFÉRENTE (feminine)
READY is PRÊT (masculine), PRÊTE (feminine)
DARK is BRUN (masculine), BRUNE (feminine)
ELEGANT is ÉLÉGANT (masculine), ÉLÉGANTE (feminine)
HAPPY is HEUREUX (masculine), HEUREUSE (feminine)

The other words you have just learned are the same in the masculine and in the feminine.

19

## SOME VERBS

### THINK OF EACH IMAGE IN YOUR MIND'S EYE FOR ABOUT TEN SECONDS

○ The French for I WRITE is J'ÉCRIS
Imagine saying, 'I AGREE to WRITE to you.'

○ The French for I AM SITTING (I AM SEATED) is
JE SUIS ASSIS
Imagine saying, 'I SEE I am SITTING.'

○ The French for I SERVE is JE SERS
Imagine saying, 'SIR, can I SERVE you?'

○ The French for I ANSWER is JE RÉPONDS
Imagine saying, 'RESPOND! ANSWER me!'

○ The French for I ASK is JE DEMANDE
Imagine I DEMAND that you ASK a question.

## YOU CAN WRITE YOUR ANSWERS IN

○ What is the English for JE DEMANDE?  _____

○ What is the English for JE RÉPONDS?  _____

○ What is the English for JE SERS?  _____

○ What is the English for JE SUIS ASSIS?  _____

○ What is the English for J'ÉCRIS?  _____

TURN BACK FOR THE ANSWERS

## COVER UP THE LEFT HAND PAGE

○ What is the French for I ask? _____

○ What is the French for I answer? _____

○ What is the French for I serve? _____

○ What is the French for I am sitting? _____

○ What is the French for I write? _____

TURN BACK FOR THE ANSWERS

## ELEMENTARY GRAMMAR

When you ASK or ANSWER somebody, for example,

> I ASK  MY  AUNT, or
> I ANSWER  MY  UNCLE,

then in French the sentence takes the form:

> I ASK *TO* MY AUNT, or
> I ANSWER *TO* MY UNCLE.

So,

> I ASK MY AUNT  is  JE DEMANDE À MA TANTE
> I ANSWER MY UNCLE  is  JE RÉPONDS À MON ONCLE

Now cover up the answers below and translate the following:

(You can write your answers in)

1. I SERVE THE HAPPY PEOPLE AND THE
   WELL-BEHAVED AUNT

2. I AM SITTING HERE BUT YOU WANT THE
   TELEPHONE AND I ASK THE BRIDE

3. THE FAMILY SEES A HUMAN BEING, BUT HE IS
   ALONE WITH THE GRANDSON

4. THE BRIDE IS VERY DIFFERENT. SHE IS DARK AND
   ELEGANT AND IS A COUSIN. SHE IS VERY POPULAR

5. I ANSWER YOUR POOR UNCLE AND I AM WRITING
   A SINCERE LETTER

The answers are:

1. JE SERS LES GENS HEUREUX ET LA TANTE SAGE

2. JE SUIS ASSIS ICI MAIS VOUS VOULEZ LE
   TÉLÉPHONE ET JE DEMANDE À L'ÉPOUSE
   (N.B. A female would say JE SUIS ASSI*SE*)

3. LA FAMILLE VOIT UN ÊTRE HUMAIN, MAIS IL EST
   SEUL AVEC LE PETIT-FILS

4. L'ÉPOUSE EST TRÈS DIFFÉRENTE. ELLE EST
   BRUNE ET ÉLÉGANTE ET EST UNE COUSINE. ELLE
   EST TRÈS POPULAIRE

5. JE RÉPONDS À VOTRE PAUVRE ONCLE ET
   J'ÉCRIS UNE LETTRE SINCÈRE

**Note**
In the last sentence the word for POOR came before the noun. This
happens when PAUVRE means 'unfortunate' rather than 'having
no money'.

## ELEMENTARY GRAMMAR

To say second, third, fourth, fifth, and so on, you simply add
–IÈME to the number (the spelling sometimes changes a little).

So,

> THE THIRD DOG  is  LE TROISIÈME CHIEN
>
> THE FIFTH HOUSE  is  LA CINQUIÈME MAISON

The only exception is FIRST which is:

> PREMIER  in  the masculine
>
> PREMIÈRE  in  the feminine.

Now cover up the answers below and translate the following:

(You can write your answers in)

1. THE UNCLE'S GRANDSON IS NOT MY COUSIN
2. THE POOR DOG IS READY, BUT I AM WRITING A SECOND BOOK
3. THE FIRST BRIDE'S RELATION IS VERY POOR AND SHE IS ALONE
4. MY UNCLE'S CAT IS VERY WELL BEHAVED AND EATS THE PEOPLE
5. MY (FEMALE) COUSIN'S HORSE IS VERY BLACK AND VERY FAST

The answers are

1. LE PETIT-FILS DE L'ONCLE N'EST PAS MON COUSIN
2. LE PAUVRE CHIEN EST PRÊT, MAIS J'ÉCRIS UN DEUXIÈME LIVRE
3. LE PARENT DE LA PREMIÈRE ÉPOUSE EST TRÈS PAUVRE ET ELLE EST SEULE
4. LE CHAT DE MON ONCLE EST TRÈS SAGE ET MANGE LES GENS
5. LE CHEVAL DE MA COUSINE EST TRÈS NOIR ET TRÈS RAPIDE

## IMPORTANT NOTE

Some of the sentences in this course might strike you as being a bit odd!

However, they have been carefully constructed to make you think much more about what you are translating. This helps the memory process and gets away from the idea of learning useful phrases 'parrot fashion'.

But of course, having learned with the help of these seemingly odd sentences, you can easily construct your own sentences to suit your particular needs. However, from time to time during the course, more 'sensible' sentences will be given for you to translate in order to show you how your knowledge can be applied to deal with every-day situations.

## BOAT WORDS

### THINK OF EACH IMAGE IN YOUR MIND'S EYE FOR ABOUT TEN SECONDS

○ The French for ANCHOR is ANCRE
Imagine throwing an ANCHOR from the top of the Eiffel Tower.

○ The French for QUAY is QUAI
Imagine building a replica Eiffel Tower on a QUAY side.

○ The French for CLIFF is FALAISE
Imagine someone who FALLS over a cliff.

○ The French for DINGHY is CANOT
Imagine your dinghy sinking a CANOE.

○ The French for LIFE BELT is CEINTURE DE SAUVETAGE
Imagine a lifebelt marks a CENTRE OF SABOTAGE.

○ The French for OAR is RAME
Imagine you RAM an oar in someone's stomach.

○ The French for SAIL is VOILE
Imagine you FILL a sail with wind.

○ The French for SAILOR is MARIN
Imagine a sailor is a MARINER.

○ The French for SEAGULL is MOUETTE
Imagine if you want to frighten a seagull, you should get a cow to MOO IT away.

○ The French for TIDE is MARÉE
Imagine you should always MARRY when the tide is high.

# YOU CAN WRITE YOUR ANSWERS IN

○ What is the English for MARÉE? _____

○ What is the English for MOUETTE? _____

○ What is the English for MARIN? _____

○ What is the English for VOILE? _____

○ What is the English for RAME? _____

○ What is the English for CEINTURE DE
SAUVETAGE? _____

○ What is the English for CANOT? _____

○ What is the English for FALAISE? _____

○ What is the English for QUAI? _____

○ What is the English for ANCRE? _____

## TURN BACK FOR THE ANSWERS

# GENDERS

## THINK OF EACH IMAGE IN YOUR MIND'S EYE FOR ABOUT TEN SECONDS

○ The gender of ANCHOR is FEMININE          L'ANCRE (f)
   Imagine throwing a bottle of perfume at an
   anchor.

○ The gender of QUAY is MASCULINE          LE QUAI
   Imagine boxers fighting on the quayside.

○ The gender of CLIFF is FEMININE          LA FALAISE
   Imagine pouring perfume over a cliff.

○ The gender of DINGHY is MASCULINE          LE CANOT
   Imagine a boxer sailing a dinghy.

○ The gender of LIFE BELT is FEMININE          LA CEINTURE
                                                DE SAUVETAGE

   Imagine throwing a lifebelt into a pool
   of perfume.

○ The gender of OAR is FEMININE          LA RAME
   Imagine dipping your oar in perfume.

○ The gender of SAIL is FEMININE          LA VOILE
   Imagine washing sails in perfume.

○ The gender of SAILOR is MASCULINE          LE MARIN
   Imagine a boxer punching a sailor.

○ The gender of SEAGULL is FEMININE          LA MOUETTE
   Imagine a seagull drinking from a bottle of
   perfume.

○ The gender of TIDE is FEMININE          LA MARÉE
   Imagine the tide washing up bottles of
   perfume.

## YOU CAN WRITE YOUR ANSWERS IN

○ What is the gender and French for tide? _____

○ What is the gender and French for seagull? _____

○ What is the gender and French for sailor? _____

○ What is the gender and French for sail? _____

○ What is the gender and French for OAR? _____

○ What is the gender and French for life belt? _____

○ What is the gender and French for dinghy? _____

○ What is the gender and French for cliff? _____

○ What is the gender and French for quay? _____

○ What is the gender and French for anchor? _____

## TURN BACK FOR THE ANSWERS

Now cover up the answers below and translate the following:

(You can write your answers in)

1. THE GRANDSON'S FOURTH ANCHOR IS ON THE CLIFF
2. THE TIDE IS HIGH AND HE WANTS THE DINGHY
3. THE LIFEBELT IS HERE AND THE OARS ARE ON THE QUAY
4. I AM ALONE, AND I WRITE A LETTER ON THE SAIL
5. I ASK THE SAILOR. HE SEES THE ELEGANT SEAGULL

The answers are:

1. LA QUATRIÈME ANCRE DU PETIT-FILS EST SUR LA FALAISE
2. LA MARÉE EST HAUTE ET IL VEUT LE CANOT
3. LA CEINTURE DE SAUVETAGE EST ICI ET LES RAMES SONT SUR LE QUAI
4. JE SUIS SEUL ET J'ÉCRIS UNE LETTRE SUR LA VOILE (N.B. A female would say JE SUIS SEULE)
5. JE DEMANDE AU MARIN. IL VOIT LA MOUETTE ÉLÉGANTE

Please note: In the last sentence you may have put À LE in front of MARIN. When À and LE come together, they become AU.

## Section 2   TOWN AND TRAVELLING

### TOWN AND CITY WORDS

### THINK OF EACH IMAGE IN YOUR MIND'S EYE FOR ABOUT TEN SECONDS

○ The French for CATHEDRAL is CATHÉDRALE
   Imagine the Eiffel Tower towering like a CATHEDRAL.

○ The French for CORNER is COIN
   Imagine a CHOIR standing on a corner.

○ The French for TOLL is PÉAGE
   Imagine thinking that tolls are for PAY AS you go.

○ The French for QUEUE is QUEUE
   Imagine you QUEUE to get into the Eiffel Tower.

○ The French for STREET is RUE
   Imagine people being RUde in the street.

○ The French for BUILDING is BÂTIMENT
   Imagine looking at the BATTLEMENTS of an old building.

○ The French for CITIZEN is CITOYEN
   Imagine telling an old citizen, 'I would like to SIT ON YA!'

○ The French for TOWN SQUARE is PLACE
   Imagine that the PLACE to be is the town square.

○ The French for TOWN HALL is MAIRIE
   Imagine MARY Queen of Scots addressing her people from the town hall.

○ The French for STADIUM is STADE
   Imagine saying, 'IS DAD at the stadium?'

## YOU CAN WRITE YOUR ANSWERS IN

○ What is the English for STADE? _____

○ What is the English for MAIRIE? _____

○ What is the English for PLACE? _____

○ What is the English for CITOYEN? _____

○ What is the English for BÂTIMENT? _____

○ What is the English for RUE? _____

○ What is the English for QUEUE? _____

○ What is the English for PÉAGE? _____

○ What is the English for COIN? _____

○ What is the English for CATHÉDRALE? _____

## TURN BACK FOR THE ANSWERS

## GENDERS

## THINK OF EACH IMAGE IN YOUR MIND'S EYE FOR ABOUT TEN SECONDS

○ The gender of CATHEDRAL is     LA CATHÉDRALE
FEMININE
Imagine spraying a cathedral with
perfume from an aeroplane.

○ The gender of CORNER is MASCULINE     LE COIN
Imagine a boxing match on a street corner.

○ The gender of TOLL is MASCULINE     LE PÉAGE
Imagine a boxer at a toll.

○ The gender of QUEUE is FEMININE     LA QUEUE
Imagine spraying perfume over a bus
queue.

○ The gender of STREET is FEMININE     LA RUE
Imagine spraying a street with perfume.

○ The gender of BUILDING is     LE BÂTIMENT
MASCULINE
Imagine a boxer jumping off a building.

○ The gender of CITIZEN is MASCULINE     LE CITOYEN
Imagine a boxer challenging all the citizens
to a fight.

○ The gender of TOWN SQUARE is FEMININE     LA PLACE
Imagine selling bottles of perfume in the
town square.

○ The gender of TOWN HALL is FEMININE     LA MAIRIE
Imagine cleaners using perfume to clean
the town hall.

○ The gender of STADIUM is MASCULINE     LE STADE
Imagine a boxing match in a huge stadium.

## YOU CAN WRITE YOUR ANSWERS IN

○ What is the gender and French for stadium?
_____

○ What is the gender and French for town hall?
_____

○ What is the gender and French for town square?
_____

○ What is the gender and French for citizen?
_____

○ What is the gender and French for building?
_____

○ What is the gender and French for street?
_____

○ What is the gender and French for queue?
_____

○ What is the gender and French for toll?
_____

○ What is the gender and French for corner?
_____

○ What is the gender and French for cathedral?
_____

TURN BACK FOR THE ANSWERS

## SOME ADJECTIVES

## THINK OF EACH IMAGE IN YOUR MIND'S EYE FOR ABOUT TEN SECONDS

○ The French for ENDLESS is ÉTERNEL
  Imagine something that is ENDLESS and ETERNAL.

○ The French for SERIOUS (of illness) is GRAVE
  Imagine someone's illness is so SERIOUS that they are
  preparing his GRAVE!

○ The French for SERIOUS (not funny) is SÉRIEUX
  Imagine someone asking 'SIR, ARE YOU SERIOUS about
  this?'

○ The French for LAZY is PARESSEUX
  Imagine someone so LAZY that he can't be bothered to open
  his PARACHUTE.

○ The French for DISTANT is LOINTAIN
  Imagine *London* seems a DISTANT town.

○ The French for FIRM is FERME
  Imagine that the Eiffel Tower looks FIRM.

○ The French for FLAT is PLAT
  Imagine PLAnning a FLAT world.

○ The French for CHEEKY is INSOLENT
  Imagine you take a CHEEKY and INSOLENT child up the
  Eiffel Tower.

○ The French for CLEAR is CLAIR
  Imagine a CLEAR view of the eiffel tower.

○ The French for SMOOTH is LISSE
  Imagine that processing a LEASE for your house goes very
  SMOOTHLY.

## YOU CAN WRITE YOUR ANSWERS IN

○ What is the English for LISSE? _____

○ What is the English for CLAIR? _____

○ What is the English for INSOLENT? _____

○ What is the English for PLAT? _____

○ What is the English for FERME? _____

○ What is the English for LOINTAIN? _____

○ What is the English for PARESSEUX? _____

○ What is the English for SÉRIEUX? _____ (not funny)

○ What is the English for GRAVE? _____ (of illness)

○ What is the English for ÉTERNEL? _____

TURN BACK FOR THE ANSWERS

## COVER UP THE LEFT HAND PAGE

○ What is the French for smooth?  _____

○ What is the French for clear?  _____

○ What is the French for cheeky?  _____

○ What is the French for flat?  _____

○ What is the French for firm?  _____

○ What is the French for distant?  _____

○ What is the French for lazy?  _____

○ What is the French for serious (not funny)?  _____

○ What is the French for serious (of illness)?  _____

○ What is the French for endless?  _____

TURN BACK FOR THE ANSWERS

**Note**
For the words you have just learned:

SERIOUS is SÉRIEUX (masculine), SÉRIEUSE (feminine)
LAZY is PARESSEUX (masculine), PARESSEUSE (feminine)
DISTANT is LOINTAIN (masculine), LOINTAINE (feminine)
FLAT is PLAT (masculine), PLATE (feminine)
CHEEKY is INSOLENT (masculine), INSOLENTE (feminine)

The other words you have just learned are the same in the masculine and in the feminine.

## SOME USEFUL VERBS

○ The French for I CATCH is J'ATTRAPPE
  Imagine I CATCH animals in a TRAP

○ The French for I BELIEVE is JE CROIS
  Imagine I BELIEVE anything a CROW tells me

○ The French for I HATE is JE HAIS
  Imagine it is an Error to HATE someone

○ The French for I LOSE is JE PERDS
  Imagine I LOSE a PAIR of shoes

## YOU CAN WRITE YOUR ANSWERS IN

○ What is the English for JE PERDS? _____

○ What is the English for JE HAIS? _____

○ What is the English for JE CROIS? _____

○ What is the English for J'ATTRAPPE? _____

TURN BACK FOR THE ANSWERS

# COVER UP THE LEFT HAND PAGE

○ What is the French for I lose? _____

○ What is the French for I hate? _____

○ What is the French for I believe? _____

○ What is the French for I catch? _____

## TURN BACK FOR THE ANSWERS

Now cover up the answers below and translate the following:

(You can write your answers in)

1. I LOSE THE BIG QUEUE, BUT I DO NOT HATE THE CLEAR BUILDINGS

2. I SERVE THE SERIOUS AUNT, BUT I BELIEVE THE CHEEKY GRANDSON

3. I CATCH THE LAZY BRIDE. SHE IS SERIOUSLY ILL

4. I HATE THE WHITE TOWN, THE QUEUES, THE SMOOTH CORNERS AND THE DISTANT STREET

5. THE TOWN SQUARE IS FLAT, BUT THE STADIUM IS VERY BIG AND VERY FIRM

The answers are:

1. JE PERDS LA GRANDE QUEUE, MAIS JE NE HAIS PAS LES BÂTIMENTS CLAIRS

2. JE SERS LA TANTE SÉRIEUSE, MAIS JE CROIS LE PETIT-FILS INSOLENT

3. J'ATTRAPPE L'ÉPOUSE PARESSEUSE. ELLE EST GRAVEMENT MALADE (N.B. the FEMININE ending of words which end in 'x' is usually '-SE')

4. JE HAIS LA VILLE BLANCHE, LES QUEUES, LES COINS LISSES ET LA RUE LOINTAINE

5. LA PLACE EST PLATE, MAIS LE STADE EST TRÈS GRAND ET TRÈS FERME

## ELEMENTARY GRAMMAR

If you want to say sentences such as

> THE DOG IS GREENER,

in French you almost always say:

> THE DOG IS MORE GREEN.

The French for MORE is PLUS

> Imagine the sky is MORE BLUE than I ever imagined.

So,

> THE DOG IS GREENER is LE CHIEN EST PLUS VERT

There are one or two exceptions. For example:

GOOD is BON but BETTER (which is 'more good') is MEILLEUR.

> Imagine the MAYOR is BETTER.

The word for THAN is QUE.

So,

> THE DOG IS GREENER  is  LE CHIEN EST PLUS
> THAN THE CAT      VERT QUE LE CHAT

Now cover up the answers below and translate the following:

(You can write your answers in)

1. THE CITIZEN IS CHEEKIER THAN THE LAZY GIRL

2. THE TOWN HALL IS BIGGER, BUT THE STADIUM IS SMALLER THAN THE TOWN SQUARE

3. THE STREET IS FLATTER THAN THE BUILDING

4. THE AUNT IS DIRTIER AND BETTER THAN THE UNCLE

5. THE TOLL IS IN THE TOWN, AND NOT ON THE BRIDGE

The answers are:

1. LE CITOYEN EST PLUS INSOLENT QUE LA JEUNE FILLE PARESSEUSE

2. LA MAIRIE EST PLUS GRANDE, MAIS LE STADE EST PLUS PETIT QUE LA PLACE

3. LA RUE EST PLUS PLATE QUE LE BÂTIMENT

4. LA TANTE EST PLUS SALE ET MEILLEURE QUE L'ONCLE

5. LE PÉAGE EST DANS LA VILLE, ET PAS SUR LE PONT

# ON THE ROAD

## THINK OF EACH IMAGE IN YOUR MIND'S EYE FOR ABOUT TEN SECONDS

○ The French for CROSSROADS is CARREFOUR
Imagine you need a CAR FOR getting over crossroads.

○ The French for REGION is RÉGION
Imagine all French REGIONS have their own Eiffel Towers.

○ The French for OUTSKIRTS (of town) is FAUBOURG
Imagine you can't FORBEAR to live in the outskirts.

○ The French for (road) TRAFFIC is CIRCULATION
Imagine watching traffic CIRCULATING.

○ The French for ROUNDABOUT is ROND-POINT
Imagine a roundabout is a ROUND POINT.

○ The French for PASSENGER is PASSAGER
Imagine taking boat PASSENGERS to see the Eiffel Tower.

○ The French for MOTORWAY is AUTOROUTE
Imagine a motorway is a main AUTOROUTE.

○ The French for PEDESTRIAN CROSSING is PASSAGE
À PIÉTON
Imagine a pedestrian crossing is a PASSAGE for pedestrians.

○ The French for SIGNPOST is POTEAU INDICATEUR
Imagine a signpost has a PHOTO INDICATOR to help tourists.

○ The French for (the) UNDERGROUND is MÉTRO
Imagine underground railways are in the METROpolitan areas.

# YOU CAN WRITE YOUR ANSWERS IN

○ What is the English for MÉTRO? _____

○ What is the English for POTEAU INDICATEUR? _____

○ What is the English for PASSAGE À PIÉTON? _____

○ What is the English for AUTOROUTE? _____

○ What is the English for PASSAGER? _____

○ What is the English for ROND-PONT? _____

○ What is the English for CIRCULATION? _____

○ What is the English for FAUBOURG? _____

○ What is the English for RÉGION? _____

○ What is the English for CARREFOUR? _____

## TURN BACK FOR THE ANSWERS

# GENDERS

## THINK OF EACH IMAGE IN YOUR MIND'S EYE FOR ABOUT TEN SECONDS

○ The gender for CROSSROADS     LE CARREFOUR
is MASCULINE
Imagine a boxer's car stuck at a crossroads.

○ The gender for REGION is FEMININE     LA RÉGION
Imagine a region in France which
specializes in selling perfume.

○ The gender for OUTSKIRTS (of town)     LE FAUBOURG
is MASCULINE
Imagine boxers gathering on the outskirts
of a town.

○ The gender for (road) TRAFFIC     LA CIRCULATION
is FEMININE
Imagine traffic being sprayed with
perfume.

○ The gender for ROUNDABOUT     LE ROND-POINT
is MASCULINE
Imagine boxers going round and round a
roundabout.

○ The gender for PASSENGER is     LE PASSAGER
MASCULINE
Imagine boxers are passengers in a bus.

○ The gender for MOTORWAY is     L'AUTOROUTE (f)
FEMININE
Imagine perfume spilled all over the
motorway.

○ The gender for PEDESTRIAN CROSSING     LE PASSAGE
is MASCULINE     À PIÉTON
Imagine boxers waiting to cross a
pedestrian crossing.

○ The gender for SIGNPOST     LE POTEAU INDICATEUR
is MASCULINE
Imagine a boxer perched on top of a
signpost.

○ The gender for (the) UNDERGROUND     LE MÉTRO
is MASCULINE
Imagine boxers sitting on an underground
train.

# YOU CAN WRITE YOUR ANSWERS IN

○ What is the gender and French for underground?
_____

○ What is the gender and French for sign post?
_____

○ What is the gender and French for pedestrian crossing?
_____

○ What is the gender and French for motorway?
_____

○ What is the gender and French for passenger?
_____

○ What is the gender and French for roundabout?
_____

○ What is the gender and French for road traffic?
_____

○ What is the gender and French for outskirts (of town)?
_____

○ What is the gender and French for region?
_____

○ What is the gender and French for crossroads?
_____

## TURN BACK FOR THE ANSWERS

Now cover up the answers below and translate the following:

(You can write the answers in)

1. THE PEDESTRIAN IS DIRTIER THAN THE
   PASSENGER
2. THE REGION IS FLATTER THAN THE MOTORWAY
3. THE SIGNPOST IS IN THE UNDERGROUND
4. I HATE THE TRAFFIC MORE THAN THE
   ROUNDABOUT
5. SHE SEES THE DISTANT CROSSROADS
   AND THE SMOOTH OUTSKIRTS

The answers are:

1. LE PIÉTON EST PLUS SALE QUE LE PASSAGER
2. LA RÉGION EST PLUS PLATE QUE L'AUTOROUTE
3. LE POTEAU INDICATEUR EST DANS LE MÉTRO
4. JE HAIS LA CIRCULATION PLUS QUE LE
   ROND-POINT
5. ELLE VOIT LE CARREFOUR LOINTAIN ET LES
   FOUBOURGS LISSES

## Section 3   TRAVELLING AND FOOD

**TRAVELLING**

## THINK OF EACH IMAGE IN YOUR MIND'S EYE FOR ABOUT TEN SECONDS

○ The French for FLIGHT is VOL
Imagine you FALL from your flight.

○ The French for TOURIST is TOURISTE
Imagine TOURISTS on top of the Eiffel Tower.

○ The French for AIR is AIR
Imagine breathing in the AIR at the top of the Eiffel Tower.

○ The French for TAKE-OFF is ENVOL
Imagine someone striking an ANVIL to signal take-off.

○ The French for LANDING is ATTERRISSAGE
Imagine a plane making a landing on A TERRACE.

○ The French for JOURNEY is VOYAGE
Imagine wishing someone 'bon VOYAGE' as they leave for a long journey.

○ The French for RAILWAY is CHEMIN DE FER
Imagine a ticket collector on the railway saying 'YEH, MEN, DE FARE!'

○ The French for LIFT is ASCENSEUR
Imagine A CENSOR who stops you using the lift.

○ The French for GANGWAY is PASSERELLE
Imagine someone shouting to you on a crowded gangway 'PASS HER, HELL, she's in the way!'

○ The French for PLATFORM is quai
Imagine someone saying 'OK, you can stand on the platform.'

**Note**
Platform and quay are the same in French.

## YOU CAN WRITE YOUR ANSWERS IN

○ What is the English for QUAI? _____

○ What is the English for PASSERELLE? _____

○ What is the English for ASCENSEUR? _____

○ What is the English for CHEMIN DE FER? _____

○ What is the English for VOYAGE? _____

○ What is the English for ATTERRISSAGE? _____

○ What is the English for ENVOL? _____

○ What is the English for AIR? _____

○ What is the English for TOURISTE? _____

○ What is the English for VOL? _____

TURN BACK FOR THE ANSWERS

## GENDERS

### THINK OF EACH IMAGE IN YOUR MIND'S EYE FOR ABOUT TEN SECONDS

○ The gender of FLIGHT is MASCULINE      LE VOL
Imagine a drunken boxer on your flight.

○ The gender of TOURIST is MASCULINE      LE TOURISTE
Imagine a group of boxers as tourists.

○ The gender of AIR is MASCULINE      L'AIR (m)
Imagine a boxer gulping air.

○ The gender of TAKE-OFF is MASCULINE      L'ENVOL (m)
Imagine a group of boxers preparing for
take-off.

○ The gender of LANDING is      L'ATTERRISSAGE (m)
MASCULINE
Imagine a group of boxers preparing
for landing.

○ The gender of JOURNEY is MASCULINE      LE VOYAGE
Imagine a boxer going on a journey to
bring back a title.

○ The gender of RAILWAY is      LE CHEMIN DE FER
MASCULINE
Imagine boxers all over the railway.

○ The gender of LIFT is MASCULINE      L'ASCENSEUR (m)
Imagine boxers fighting in a lift.

○ The gender of GANGWAY is      LA PASSERELLE
FEMININE
Imagine spraying perfume all over a
gangway.

○ The gender of PLATFORM is MASCULINE      LE QUAI
Imagine boxers standing on the platform.

# YOU CAN WRITE YOUR ANSWERS IN

○ What is the gender and French for
platform?
_____

○ What is the gender and French for
gangway?
_____

○ What is the gender and French for lift?
_____

○ What is the gender and French for railway?
_____

○ What is the gender and French for journey?
_____

○ What is the gender and French for landing?
_____

○ What is the gender and French for take-off?
_____

○ What is the gender and French for air?
_____

○ What is the gender and French for tourist?
_____

○ What is the gender and French for flight?
_____

## TURN BACK FOR THE ANSWERS

## SOME ADJECTIVES

## THINK OF EACH IMAGE IN YOUR MIND'S EYE FOR ABOUT TEN SECONDS

○ The French for STRAIGHT is DROIT
Imagine trying to DRAW a STRAIGHT line.

○ The French for URGENT is URGENT
Imagine it is URGENT that you get to the Eiffel Tower.

○ The French for MAIN is PRINCIPAL
Imagine trying to put forward the MAIN, the PRINCIPAL argument.

○ The French for VIOLENT is VIOLENT
Imagine someone being VIOLENT up the Eiffel Tower.

○ The French for PALE is PÂLE
Imagine the Eiffel Tower going PALE.

○ The French for WONDERFUL is MERVEILLEUX
Imagine thinking 'It's WONDERFUL, it's MARVELLOUS.'

○ The French for INTELLIGENT is INTELLIGENT
Imagine thinking how INTELLIGENT it was to invent the Eiffel Tower.

○ The French for COOL is FRAIS
Imagine that you can FRY ice-cream when it is COOL.

○ The French for BORING is ENNUYEUX
Imagine telling someone, 'ON WITH YOU, you're so BORING!'

○ The French for OPEN is OUVERT
Imagine using a HOOVER to OPEN a door.

## YOU CAN WRITE YOUR ANSWERS IN

○ What is the English for OUVERT? _____

○ What is the English for ENNUYEUX? _____

○ What is the English for FRAIS? _____

○ What is the English for INTELLIGENT? _____

○ What is the English for MERVEILLEUX? _____

○ What is the English for PÂLE? _____

○ What is the English for VIOLENT? _____

○ What is the English for PRINCIPAL? _____

○ What is the English for URGENT? _____

○ What is the English for DROIT? _____

## TURN BACK FOR THE ANSWERS

# COVER UP THE LEFT HAND PAGE

○ What is the French for open? _____

○ What is the French for boring? _____

○ What is the French for cool? _____

○ What is the French for intelligent? _____

○ What is the French for wonderful? _____

○ What is the French for pale? _____

○ What is the French for violent? _____

○ What is the French for principal? _____

○ What is the French for urgent? _____

○ What is the French for straight? _____

## TURN BACK FOR THE ANSWERS

**Note**
For the words you have just learned

STRAIGHT is DROIT (masculine), DROITE (feminine)
URGENT is URGENT (masculine), URGENTE (feminine)
VIOLENT is VIOLENT (masculine), VIOLENTE (feminine)
WONDERFUL is MERVEILLEUX (masculine), MERVEIL-
LEUSE (feminine)
INTELLIGENT is INTELLIGENT (masculine), INTELLI-
GENTE (feminine)
COOL is FRAIS (masculine), FRAÎCHE (feminine)
BORING is ENNUYEUX (masculine), ENNUYEUSE (feminine)
OPEN is OUVERT (masculine), OUVERTE (feminine)

The other words you have just learned are the same in the masculine and in the feminine.

## SOME USEFUL VERBS

## THINK OF EACH IMAGE IN YOUR MIND'S EYE FOR ABOUT TEN SECONDS

○ The French for I READ is JE LIS
  Imagine you LEAn over whenever you READ a book.

○ The French for I SAY is JE DIS
  Imagine I SAY 'D' three times – 'D, D, D . . .'

○ The French for I SLEEP is JE DORS
  Imagine the DOOR is always open when I SLEEP.

○ The French for I PUT is JE METS
  Imagine asking if I MAY PUT something on the table.

## YOU CAN WRITE YOUR ANSWERS IN

○ What is the English for JE METS? _____

○ What is the English for JE DORS? _____

○ What is the English for JE DIS? _____

○ What is the English for JE LIS? _____

TURN BACK FOR THE ANSWERS

66

## COVER UP THE LEFT HAND PAGE

○ What is the French for I put? _____

○ What is the French for I sleep? _____

○ What is the French for I say? _____

○ What is the French for I read? _____

**TURN BACK FOR THE ANSWERS**

Now cover up the answers below and translate the following:

(You can write your answers in)

1. THE FLIGHT IS WONDERFUL; I READ MY BOOK AND I SLEEP

2. THE GRANDSON IS A PALE TOURIST

3. I SAY, 'NO, THE JOURNEY IS BORING'

4. THE LIFT IS OPEN, AND I PUT MY BOOK ON THE SUITCASE

5. THE MAIN PLATFORM OF THE STATION IS VERY STRAIGHT

The answers are:

1. LE VOL EST MERVEILLEUX; JE LIS MON LIVRE ET JE DORS

2. LE PETIT-FILS EST UN TOURISTE PÂLE

3. JE DIS, 'NON, LE VOYAGE EST ENNUYEUX'

4. L'ASCENSEUR EST OUVERT, ET JE METS MON LIVRE SUR LA VALISE

5. LE QUAI PRINCIPAL DE LA GARE EST TRÈS DROIT

## ELEMENTARY GRAMMAR

To say I AM GOING TO in French, in sentences like I AM GOING TO EAT, you use JE VAIS for I AM GOING.

Imagine a German saying, 'I AM GOING on my VAY now.'

To say I AM GOING TO EAT you say JE VAIS MANGER

In the majority of cases, the verb at the end of the sentence (for example 'to eat') will be pronounced in the same way as when you use the verb with YOU, as in YOU EAT, though the spelling is different.

For example,

    (VOUS) MANGEZ  :  MANGER
        (you eat)       (to eat)

    (VOUS) PARLEZ  :  PARLER
        (you speak)    (to speak)

Exceptions will be indicated in the course. Here are some useful ones:

    I AM GOING TO SLEEP  is  JE VAIS DORMIR

    I AM GOING TO READ  is  JE VAIS LIRE

     I AM GOING TO SEE  is  JE VAIS VOIR

Now cover up the answers below and translate the following:

(You can write your answers in)

1. I AM GOING TO SLEEP ON THE GANGWAY
2. I AM GOING TO READ AT THE STATION
3. THE TAKE-OFF WAS VIOLENT, THE AIR WAS COOL, BUT THE LANDING WAS BORING
4. I AM GOING TO EAT THE AIR
5. I AM GOING TO SEE THE RAILWAY AND THE INTELLIGENT DOCTOR

The answers are:

1. JE VAIS DORMIR SUR LA PASSERELLE
2. JE VAIS LIRE À LA GARE
3. L'ENVOL ÉTAIT VIOLENT, L'AIR ÉTAIT FRAIS, MAIS L'ATTERRISSAGE ÉTAIT ENNUYEUX
4. JE VAIS MANGER L'AIR
5. JE VAIS VOIR LE CHEMIN DE FER ET LE MÉDECIN INTELLIGENT

## FOOD WORDS

### THINK OF EACH IMAGE IN YOUR MIND'S EYE FOR ABOUT TEN SECONDS

○ The French for SANDWICH is SANDWICH
  Imagine taking SANDWICHES to eat on top of the Eiffel Tower.

○ The French for PANCAKE is CRÊPE
  Imagine a CRÊPE Suzette is a pancake.

○ The French for CIDER is CIDRE
  Imagine making cider in CEDAR-wood barrels.

○ The French for ARTICHOKE is ARTICHAUT
  Imagine artichokes are HARD TO SHOW.

○ The French for ASPARAGUS is ASPERGE
  Imagine casting ASPERSIONS on your asparagus.

○ The French for FRENCH BREAD is BAGUETTE
  Imagine when you buy French bread you should BAG IT at once.

○ The French for TOAST is PAIN GRILLÉ
  Imagine you make toast in a PAN, GREY with age.

○ The French for VINEGAR is VINAIGRE
  Imagine pouring VINEGAR from the top of the Eiffel Tower.

○ The French for STARTER is ENTRÉE
  Imagine making an ENTRY with a marvellous starter for a meal.

○ The French for VEAL is VEAU
  Imagine feeding your FOE poisoned veal.

## YOU CAN WRITE YOUR ANSWERS IN

○ What is the English for VEAU? _____

○ What is the English for ENTRÉE? _____

○ What is the English for VINAIGRE? _____

○ What is the English for PAIN GRILLÉ? _____

○ What is the English for BAGUETTE? _____

○ What is the English for ASPERGE? _____

○ What is the English for ARTICHAUT? _____

○ What is the English for CIDRE? _____

○ What is the English for CRÊPE? _____

○ What is the English for SANDWICH? _____

TURN BACK FOR THE ANSWERS

## GENDERS

**THINK OF EACH IMAGE IN YOUR MIND'S EYE FOR ABOUT TEN SECONDS**

○ The gender for SANDWICH is MASCULINE      LE SANDWICH
Imagine a boxer eating a sandwich between rounds.

○ The gender for PANCAKE is FEMININE      LA CRÊPE
Imagine pouring perfume onto your pancake.

○ The gender for CIDER is MASCULINE      LE CIDRE
Imagine a boxer getting drunk on cider.

○ The gender for ARTICHOKE is MASCULINE      L'ARTICHAUT (m)
Imagine a boxer with an artichoke sticking out of his ear.

○ The gender for ASPARAGUS is FEMININE      L'ASPERGE (f)
Imagine asparagus cooked in a perfume sauce.

○ The gender for FRENCH BREAD is FEMININE      LA BAGUETTE
Imagine finding a perfume bottle inside a French bread.

○ The gender for TOAST is MASCULINE      LE PAIN GRILLÉ
Imagine a boxer eating only toast to keep his weight down.

○ The gender for VINEGAR is MASCULINE      LE VINAIGRE
Imagine boxers bathing their cuts with vinegar.

○ The gender for STARTER is FEMININE      L'ENTRÉE (f)
Imagine drinking a glass of perfume for a starter.

○ The gender for VEAL is MASCULINE      LE VEAU
Imagine a boxer dining on a huge piece of veal.

# YOU CAN WRITE YOUR ANSWERS IN

○ What is the gender and French for veal? _____

○ What is the gender and French for starter? _____

○ What is the gender and French for vinegar? _____

○ What is the gender and French for toast? _____

○ What is the gender and French for French bread? _____

○ What is the gender and French for asparagus? _____

○ What is the gender and French for artichoke? _____

○ What is the gender and French for cider? _____

○ What is the gender and French for pancake? _____

○ What is the gender and French for sandwich? _____

## TURN BACK FOR THE ANSWERS

Now cover up the answers below and translate the following:

(You can write your answers in)

1.  I AM GOING TO EAT THE TOAST BUT I DO NOT EAT
    THE PANCAKE

2.  THE STARTER IS WONDERFUL AND I EAT IT

3.  THE CIDER AND THE ARTICHOKE WERE VIOLENT,
    BUT THE ASPARAGUS WAS PALE

4.  I SERVE THE FRENCH BREAD, BUT I DO NOT EAT
    THE SANDWICH

5.  THE VINEGAR WAS ON THE TABLE BUT THE
    FATHER'S VEAL WAS COLD

The answers are:

1.  JE VAIS MANGER LE PAIN GRILLÉ MAIS JE NE
    MANGE PAS LA CRÊPE

2.  L'ENTRÉE EST MERVEILLEUSE ET JE LA MANGE

3.  LE CIDRE ET L'ARTICHAUT ÉTAIENT VIOLENTS,
    MAIS L'ASPERGE ÉTAIT PÂLE

4.  JE SERS LA BAGUETTE, MAIS JE NE MANGE PAS LE
    SANDWICH

5.  LE VINAIGRE ÉTAIT SUR LA TABLE MAIS LE VEAU
    DU PÈRE ÉTAIT FROID

## HERE ARE SOME 'SENSIBLE' REVISION SENTENCES

1. I AM SERVING THE DINNER
2. THE RAILWAY IS WONDERFUL
3. MY DOG IS VERY LAZY
4. I SLEEP ALONE
5. I AM GOING TO ASK

The answers are:

1. JE SERS LE DÎNER
2. LE CHEMIN DE FER EST MERVEILLEUX
3. MON CHIEN EST TRÈS PARESSEUX
4. JE DORS SEUL
5. JE VAIS DEMANDER

76

Now cover up the answers below and translate the following:

(You can write your answers in)

1. MY AUNT IS SERIOUSLY ILL
2. I AM GOING TO PUT THE SUITCASE ON THE BED
3. THE CAR IS QUICKER THAN THE BOAT
4. SHE IS INTELLIGENT
5. YOUR SISTER IS VERY CHEEKY

The answers are:

1. MA TANTE EST GRAVEMENT MALADE
2. JE VAIS METTRE LA VALISE SUR LE LIT
3. L'AUTO EST PLUS RAPIDE QUE LE BATEAU
4. ELLE EST INTELLIGENTE
5. VOTRE SOEUR EST TRÈS INSOLENTE

## Section 4    WEATHER AND GARDENING

**THINK OF EACH IMAGE IN YOUR MIND'S EYE FOR ABOUT TEN SECONDS**

○ The French for WEATHER is TEMPS
   Imagine a TOM cat out in all weathers.

○ The French for BLACK ICE is VERGLAS
   Imagine a German saying, 'That black ice looked as if it VER GLASS.'

○ The French for THUNDER is TONNERRE
   Imagine putting hair TONER on to protect yourself from the thunder.

○ The French for LIGHTNING is ÉCLAIR
   Imagine lightning strikes your chocolate ECLAIR.

○ The French for FROST is GELÉE
   Imagine feeling JOLLY because frost has come.

○ The French for HAIL is GRÊLE
   Imagine trying to GRILL hail stones.

○ The French for FLOOD is DÉLUGE
   Imagine that a DELUGE of rain causes a flood.

○ The French for CLIMATE is CLIMAT
   Imagine observing the climate from the top of the Eiffel Tower.

○ The French for SKY is CIEL
   Imagine the sky is your CEILing.

○ The French for WIND is VENT
   Imagine you are very FOND of wind.

## YOU CAN WRITE YOUR ANSWERS IN

○ What is the English for VENT? _____

○ What is the English for CIEL? _____

○ What is the English for CLIMAT? _____

○ What is the English for DÉLUGE? _____

○ What is the English for GRÊLE? _____

○ What is the English for GELÉE? _____

○ What is the English for ÉCLAIR? _____

○ What is the English for TONNERRE? _____

○ What is the English for VERGLAS? _____

○ What is the English for TEMPS? _____

## TURN BACK FOR THE ANSWERS

## GENDERS

## THINK OF EACH IMAGE IN YOUR MIND'S EYE FOR ABOUT TEN SECONDS

○ The gender of WEATHER is MASCULINE
Imagine a boxer giving the weather forecast.

**LE TEMPS**

○ The gender of BLACK ICE is MASCULINE
Imagine a boxer slipping on black ice during a fight.

**LE VERGLAS**

○ The gender of THUNDER is MASCULINE
Imagine a boxer who makes a noise like thunder when he hits someone.

**LE TONNERRE**

○ The gender of LIGHTNING is MASCULINE
Imagine a boxer with a punch like lightning.

**l'ÉCLAIR (m)**

○ The gender of FROST is FEMININE
Imagine spraying perfume onto a frosty path.

**LA GELÉE**

○ The gender of HAIL is FEMININE
Imagine putting hail into a perfume bottle.

**LA GRÊLE**

○ The gender of FLOOD is MASCULINE
Imagine a boxer carried away by a flood.

**LE DÉLUGE**

○ The gender of CLIMATE is MASCULINE
Imagine boxers who hate boxing in a hot climate.

**LE CLIMAT**

○ The gender of SKY is MASCULINE
Imagine a boxer lying on the floor looking at the sky.

**LE CIEL**

○ The gender of WIND is MASCULINE
Imagine a boxer blown over by a gust of wind.

**LE VENT**

## YOU CAN WRITE YOUR ANSWERS IN

○ What is the gender and French for wind? _____

○ What is the gender and French for sky? _____

○ What is the gender and French for climate? _____

○ What is the gender and French for flood? _____

○ What is the gender and French for hail? _____

○ What is the gender and French for frost? _____

○ What is the gender and French for lightning? _____

○ What is the gender and French for thunder? _____

○ What is the gender and French for black ice? _____

○ What is the gender and French for weather? _____

TURN BACK FOR THE ANSWERS

## SOME ADJECTIVES

## THINK OF EACH IMAGE IN YOUR MIND'S EYE FOR ABOUT TEN SECONDS

○ The French for DELICIOUS is DÉLICIEUX
Imagine eating something DELICIOUS at the top of the Eiffel Tower.

○ The French for LIGHT (weight) is LÉGER
Imagine drinking something LIGHT at a LEISURELY pace.

○ The French for NEXT is PROCHAIN
Imagine the French threatening to invade PRUSSIA NEXT.

○ The French for NEW is NOUVEAU
Imagine a NEW NOVEL.

○ The French for RICH is RICHE
Imagine the idle RICH up the Eiffel Tower.

○ The French for OBVIOUS is ÉVIDENT
Imagine it is OBVIOUS, it is EVIDENT

○ The French for SUITABLE is CONVENABLE
Imagine asking if it is CONVENIENT and SUITABLE to arrange a meeting.

○ The French for RIPE is MÛR
Imagine a load of RIPE fruit scattered all over a MOOR.

○ The French for PRACTICAL is PRATIQUE
Imagine someone telling you that the Eiffel Tower is not PRACTICAL.

○ The French for CHARMING is CHARMANT
Imagine I SHARE MY things with a CHARMING girl.

## YOU CAN WRITE YOUR ANSWERS IN

○ What is the English for CHARMANT? _____

○ What is the English for PRATIQUE? _____

○ What is the English for MÛR? _____

○ What is the English for CONVENABLE? _____

○ What is the English for ÉVIDENT? _____

○ What is the English for RICHE? _____

○ What is the English for NOUVEAU? _____

○ What is the English for PROCHAIN? _____

○ What is the English for LÉGER? _____

○ What is the English for DÉLICIEUX? _____

## TURN BACK FOR THE ANSWERS

## COVER UP THE LEFT HAND PAGE

○ What is the French for charming?       _____

○ What is the French for practical?       _____

○ What is the French for ripe?       _____

○ What is the French for suitable?       _____

○ What is the French for obvious?       _____

○ What is the French for rich?       _____

○ What is the French for new?       _____

○ What is the French for next?       _____

○ What is the French for light (weight)?       _____

○ What is the French for delicious?       _____

TURN BACK FOR THE ANSWERS

**Note**
For the words you have just learned

DELICIOUS is DÉLICIEUX (masculine), DÉLICIEUSE (feminine)
LIGHT (weight) is LÉGER (masculine), LÉGÈRE (feminine)
NEXT is PROCHAIN (masculine), PROCHAINE (feminine)
NEW is NOUVEAU (masculine), NOUVELLE (feminine)
OBVIOUS is ÉVIDENT (masculine), ÉVIDENTE (feminine)
CHARMING is CHARMANT (masculine), CHARMANTE (feminine)

The other words you have just learned are the same in the masculine and in the feminine.

## SOME VERBS

## THINK OF EACH IMAGE IN YOUR MIND'S EYE FOR ABOUT TEN SECONDS

○ The French for I LIVE (reside) is J'HABITE
   Imagine that I LIVE A BIT down the road from you.

○ The French for I SHOW is JE MONTRE
   Imagine I SHOW you the Loch Ness MON(S)TER!

○ The French for I DANCE is JE DANSE
   Imagine I DANCE on top of the Eiffel Tower.

○ The French for I FIND is JE TROUVE
   Imagine I FIND a treasure TROVE.

## YOU CAN WRITE YOUR ANSWERS IN

○ What is the English for JE TROUVE? _____

○ What is the English for JE DANSE? _____

○ What is the English for JE MONTRE? _____

○ What is the English for J'HABITE? _____

**TURN BACK FOR THE ANSWERS**

# COVER UP THE LEFT HAND PAGE

○ What is the French for I find? _____

○ What is the French for I dance? _____

○ What is the French for I show? _____

○ What is the French for I live (reside)? _____

**TURN BACK FOR THE ANSWERS**

Now cover up the answers below and translate the following

(You can write your answers in)

1. THE THUNDER AND LIGHTNING ARE VERY
   VIOLENT. MY AUNT IS CHARMING AND MY COUSIN
   IS DELICIOUS

2. I LIVE IN THE COLD WATER AND MY SKIRT IS NOT
   PRACTICAL IN A COLD CLIMATE

3. I AM GOING TO SHOW THE BLACK ICE AND THE
   FROST TO THE GIRL

4. THE HAIL, THE WIND AND THE OBVIOUS FLOOD
   ARE ON THE TOWN HALL

5. I FIND THE LIGHT BOY. THE NEXT CITIZEN IS NOT
   SUITABLE. THE NEW BRIDE IS RICH

The answers are:

1. LE TONNERRE ET L'ÉCLAIR SONT TRÈS
   VIOLENTS. MA TANTE EST CHARMANTE ET MON
   COUSIN EST DÉLICIEUX

2. J'HABITE DANS L'EAU FROIDE ET MA JUPE N'EST
   PAS PRATIQUE DANS UN CLIMAT FROID

3. JE VAIS MONTRER LE VERGLAS ET LA GELÉE À
   LA JEUNE FILLE

4. LA GRÊLE, LE VENT ET LE DÉLUGE ÉVIDENT
   SONT SUR LA MAIRIE

5. JE TROUVE LE GARÇON LÉGER. LE PROCHAIN
   CITOYEN N'EST PAS CONVENABLE. LA NOUVELLE
   ÉPOUSE EST RICHE

**Note**
1. PROCHAIN often comes before the word it goes with.
2. The feminine of NOUVEAU is NOUVELLE. It also usually
comes before the word it goes with.

## ELEMENTARY GRAMMAR

In French, to say

### I ATE or I HAVE EATEN

you say

### J'AI MANGÉ.

Notice that the world MANGÉ sounds like the word you use when you say YOU EAT (VOUS MANGEZ), although it is spelled differently.

Here is another example:

### I SPOKE or I HAVE SPOKEN: J'AI PARLÉ

Many verbs work like this.

There are quite a few exceptions to the ending of the verb, but do not worry about them at this stage.

However, here is one exception worth noting now:

### I WROTE or HAVE WRITTEN: J'AI ÉCRIT

Now cover up the answers below and translate the following:

(You can write your answers in)

1. I HAVE EATEN THE RIPE FRUIT, AND I HAVE EATEN THE NEW POTATOES

2. I DANCED ON THE DIRTY BRIDGE IN THE COLD WATER

3. I SLEEP UNDER THE BLUE SKY, BUT THE BLACK ICE WAS VERY BLACK

4. I ATE THE THIN CAT

5. I CAUGHT THE WIND AND THE COLD RAIN

The answers are:

1. J'AI MANGÉ LE FRUIT MÛR, ET J'AI MANGÉ LES NOUVELLES POMMES DE TERRE

2. J'AI DANSÉ SUR LE PONT SALE DANS L'EAU FROIDE

3. JE DORS SOUS LE CIEL BLEU, MAIS LE VERGLAS ÉTAIT TRÈS NOIR

4. J'AI MANGÉ LE CHAT MINCE

5. J'AI ATTRAPPÉ LE VENT ET LA PLUIE FROIDE

## IN THE GARDEN

**THINK OF EACH IMAGE IN YOUR MIND'S EYE FOR
ABOUT TEN SECONDS**

○ The French for RAKE is RÂTEAU
Imagine hitting a RAT Over the head with a rake.

○ The French for WEED is MAUVAISE HERBE
Imagine telling someone, 'MOVE THIS HERB, it's a weed.'

○ The French for WHEELBARROW is BROUETTE
Imagine the best way to make beer is to BREW IT in a
wheelbarrow.

○ The French for BENCH IS BANC
Imagine a BONNY bench.

○ The French for SHRUB is ARBUSTE
Imagine as modest people, we hide OUR BUST behind a
shrub.

○ The French for BROOM is BALAI
Imagine Pavlova dancing with a broom in a BALLET.

○ The French for LEAF is FEUILLE
Imagine a cinema FOYER covered in leaves.

○ The French for HEDGE is HAIE
Imagine a hedge covered in HAY.

○ The French for PETAL is PÉTALE
Imagine dropping petals from the Eiffel Tower.

○ The French for LAWN is PELOUSE
Imagine saying, 'PLEASE keep off the lawn.'

## YOU CAN WRITE YOUR ANSWERS IN

○ What is the English for PELOUSE? _____

○ What is the English for PÉTALE? _____

○ What is the English for HAIE? _____

○ What is the English for FEUILLE? _____

○ What is the English for BALAI? _____

○ What is the English for ARBUSTE? _____

○ What is the English for BANC? _____

○ What is the English for BROUETTE? _____

○ What is the English for MAUVAISE HERBE? _____

○ What is the English for RÂTEAU? _____

TURN BACK FOR THE ANSWERS

94

# GENDERS

## THINK OF EACH IMAGE IN YOUR MIND'S EYE FOR ABOUT TEN SECONDS

○ The gender for RAKE is MASCULINE      LE RÂTEAU
Imagine hitting a boxer over the head with
a rake.

○ The gender for WEED is      LA MAUVAISE HERBE
FEMININE
Imagine making perfume from garden
weeds.

○ The gender for WHEELBARROW is      LA BROUETTE
FEMININE
Imagine wheeling a wheelbarrow full of
bottles of perfume.

○ The gender for BENCH is MASCULINE      LE BANC
Imagine a boxer laid out on a bench.

○ The gender for SHRUB is MASCULINE      L'ARBUSTE (m)
Imagine a boxer hiding behind a large
shrub.

○ The gender for BROOM is MASCULINE      LE BALAI
Imagine a boxer falling over a broom.

○ The gender for LEAF is FEMININE      LA FEUILLE
Imagine a leaf which smells strongly of
perfume.

○ The gender for HEDGE is FEMININE      LA HAIE
Imagine spraying your favourite hedge
with perfume.

○ The gender for PETAL is MASCULINE      LE PÉTALE
Imagine a boxer showered with rose petals.

○ The gender for LAWN is FEMININE      LA PELOUSE
Imagine a lawn covered with bottles of
perfume.

## YOU CAN WRITE YOUR ANSWERS IN

○ What is the gender and French for lawn? _____

○ What is the gender and French for petal? _____

○ What is the gender and French for hedge? _____

○ What is the gender and French for leaf? _____

○ What is the gender and French for broom? _____

○ What is the gender and French for shrub? _____

○ What is the gender and French for bench? _____

○ What is the gender and French for wheelbarrow? _____

○ What is the gender and French for weed? _____

○ What is the gender and French for rake? _____

## TURN BACK FOR THE ANSWERS

Now cover up the answers below and translate the following:

(You can write your answers in)

1. I WROTE TO THE PETAL AND TO THE LEAF

2. I ATE THE RIPE BROOM AND I HAVE SHOWN THE HEDGE TO THE WHEELBARROW

3. I FOUND THE RAKE AND I DANCED ON THE LAWN

4. THE BENCH IS CHARMING AND PRACTICAL

5. THE WEED WAS LIGHT AND THE SHRUB WAS DELICIOUS

The answers are:

1. J'AI ÉCRIT AU PÉTALE ET À LA FEUILLE

2. J'AI MANGÉ LE BALAI MÛR ET J'AI MONTRÉ LA HAIE À LA BROUETTE

3. J'AI TROUVÉ LE RÂTEAU ET J'AI DANSÉ SUR LA PELOUSE

4. LE BANC EST CHARMANT ET PRATIQUE

5. LA MAUVAISE HERBE ÉTAIT LÉGÈRE ET L'ARBUSTE ÉTAIT DÉLICIEUX.

## Section 5    TOOLS, IN THE HOUSE

**THINK OF EACH IMAGE IN YOUR MIND'S EYE FOR ABOUT TEN SECONDS**

○ The French for NAIL is CLOU
Imagine an important CLUE in a murder case is a rusty nail.

○ The French for SCREW is VIS
Imagine an argument VIS-à-vis a screw.

○ The French for ROPE is CORDE
Imagine a CORD being used as a rope to tie you up.

○ The French for DRILL is PERCEUSE
Imagine that someone with a drill PURSUES you.

○ The French for HAMMER is MARTEAU
Imagine hitting MY TOE with a hammer.

○ The French for SCISSORS is CISEAUX
Imagine a SEESAW with scissors stuck into it.

○ The French for LADDER is ÉCHELLE
Imagine an EGG SHELL on a ladder.

○ The French for SCREWDRIVER is TOURNE-VIS
Imagine someone attacking you with a screwdriver and leaving you with a TORN FACE.

○ The French for WIRE is FIL
Imagine you FEEL wire round your neck.

○ The French for SPADE is BÊCHE
Imagine you hit your BEST friend over the head with a spade.

## YOU CAN WRITE YOUR ANSWERS IN

○ What is the English for BÊCHE?  _____

○ What is the English for FIL?  _____

○ What is the English for TOURNE-VIS?  _____

○ What is the English for ÉCHELLE?  _____

○ What is the English for CISEAUX?  _____

○ What is the English for MARTEAU?  _____

○ What is the English for PERCEUSE?  _____

○ What is the English for CORDE?  _____

○ What is the English for VIS?  _____

○ What is the English for CLOU?  _____

**TURN BACK FOR THE ANSWERS**

## GENDERS

## THINK OF EACH IMAGE IN YOUR MIND'S EYE FOR ABOUT TEN SECONDS

○ The gender of NAIL is MASCULINE                LE CLOU
Imagine a boxer sitting on a nail.

○ The gender of SCREW is FEMININE                LA VIS
Imagine putting a screw in a perfume
bottle.

○ The gender of ROPE is FEMININE                LA CORDE
Imagine a perfume bottle dangling from
a rope.

○ The gender of DRILL is FEMININE                LA PERCEUSE
Imagine drilling a hole in a perfume bottle.

○ The gender of HAMMER is MASCULINE                LE MARTEAU
Imagine a boxer hitting his opponent with
a hammer.

○ The gender of SCISSORS                LES CISEAUX
is MASCULINE                (masculine plural)
Imagine a boxer cutting his gloves
with a pair of scissors.

○ The gender of LADDER is FEMININE                L'ÉCHELLE (f)
Imagine spraying a ladder with perfume.

○ The gender of SCREWDRIVER                LE TOURNE-VIS
is MASCULINE
Imagine a boxer stabbing his opponent
with a screwdriver.

○ The gender of WIRE is MASCULINE                LE FIL
Imagine a boxer tripping over a wire.

○ The gender of SPADE is FEMININE                LA BÊCHE
Imagine smashing a perfume bottle with
a spade.

## YOU CAN WRITE YOUR ANSWERS IN

○ What is the gender and French for spade?  _____

○ What is the gender and French for wire?  _____

○ What is the gender and French for screwdriver?  _____

○ What is the gender and French for ladder?  _____

○ What is the gender and French for scissors?  _____

○ What is the gender and French for hammer?  _____

○ What is the gender and French for drill?  _____

○ What is the gender and French for rope?  _____

○ What is the gender and French for screw?  _____

○ What is the gender and French for nail?  _____

## TURN BACK FOR THE ANSWERS

## SOME ADJECTIVES

### THINK OF EACH IMAGE IN YOUR MIND'S EYE FOR ABOUT TEN SECONDS

○ The French for WEAK is FAIBLE
Imagine being WEAK and FEEBLE.

○ The French for STRANGE is BIZARRE
Imagine looking STRANGE and BIZARRE.

○ The French for SURE is SÛR.
Imagine being SURE you are down a SEWER.

○ The French for STRONG is FORT
Imagine a building as STRONG as FORT Knox.

○ The French for SATISFIED is SATISFAIT
Imagine being SATISFIED with a good meal at the Eiffel Tower.

○ The French for SPECIAL is SPÉCIAL
Imagine the Eiffel Tower is something SPECIAL.

○ The French for MAD is FOU
Imagine a FOOL of a MADMAN.

○ The French for WORRIED is INQUIET
Imagine being WORRIED because you are being tied to a ship's ANCHOR.

○ The French for FORBIDDEN is INTERDIT
Imagine some food is FORBIDDEN, so you put it UNDER DE table.

○ The French for TRUE is VRAI
Imagine something that is VERY TRUE.

## YOU CAN WRITE YOUR ANSWERS IN

○ What is the English for VRAI? _____

○ What is the English for INTERDIT? _____

○ What is the English for INQUIET? _____

○ What is the English for FOU? _____

○ What is the English for SPÉCIAL? _____

○ What is the English for SATISFAIT? _____

○ What is the English for FORT? _____

○ What is the English for SÛR? _____

○ What is the English for BIZARRE? _____

○ What is the English for FAIBLE? _____

TURN BACK FOR THE ANSWERS

104

# COVER UP THE LEFT HAND PAGE

○ What is the French for true? _____

○ What is the French for forbidden? _____

○ What is the French for worried? _____

○ What is the French for mad? _____

○ What is the French for special? _____

○ What is the French for satisfied? _____

○ What is the French for strong? _____

○ What is the French for sure? _____

○ What is the French for strange? _____

○ What is the French for weak? _____

**Note**
For the words you have just learned:

STRONG is FORT (masculine), FORTE (feminine)
SATISFIED is SATISFAIT (masculine), SATISFAITE (feminine)
MAD is FOU (masculine), FOLLE (feminine)
WORRIED is INQUIET (masculine), INQUIÈTE (feminine)
FORBIDDEN is INTERDIT (masculine), INTERDITE (feminine)

The other words you have just learned are the same in the masculine and in the feminine.

**HERE ARE SOME USEFUL VERBS**

**THINK OF EACH IMAGE IN YOUR MIND'S EYE FOR ABOUT TEN SECONDS**

○ The French for I FILL is JE REMPLIS
  Imagine she FILLS a RUMPLED jersey very well.

○ The French for I HELP is J'AIDE
  Imagine I AID and HELP where I can.

○ The French for I HEAR is J'ENTENDS
  Imagine I HEAR that you like pepper ON TONGUE.

○ The French for I KISS is J'EMBRASSE
  Imagine KISSING your friend ON BRASS plates.

**YOU CAN WRITE YOUR ANSWERS IN**

○ What is the English for J'EMBRASSE? _____

○ What is the English for J'ENTENDS? _____

○ What is the English for J'AIDE? _____

○ What is the English for JE REMPLIS? _____

**TURN BACK FOR THE ANSWERS**

108

## COVER UP THE LEFT HAND PAGE

○ What is the French for I kiss? _____

○ What is the French for I hear? _____

○ What is the French for I help? _____

○ What is the French for I fill? _____

**TURN BACK FOR THE ANSWERS**

109

Now cover up the answers below and translate the following:

(You can write your answers in)

1. I KISSED THE STRANGE GIRL. SHE HAS A VERY STRONG HAMMER AND A SPECIAL POTATO.

2. I HELP THE WEAK BOY. HE WANTS THE NAILS AND THE SCREWS

3. I AM SURE AND SATISFIED. HE WANTS THE ROPE, THE SCREWDRIVER AND THE FORBIDDEN SCISSORS, BUT NOT THE LADDER

4. I KISS THE MAD DOGS AND THE THIN COWS. I AM VERY STRANGE. I AM NOT WORRIED

5. I HEAR THE DRILL AND I SEE A FULL SPADE

The answers are:

1. J'AI EMBRASSÉ LA JEUNE FILLE BIZARRE. ELLE A UN MARTEAU TRÈS FORT ET UN POMME DE TERRE SPÉCIAL

2. J'AIDE LE FAIBLE GARÇON. IL VEUT LES CLOUS ET LES VIS (N.B. FAIBLE often comes before the word it goes with)

3. JE SUIS SÛR ET SATISFAIT. IL VEUT LA CORDE, LE TOURNE-VIS ET LES CISEAUX INTERDITS MAIS PAS L'ÉCHELLE

4. J'EMBRASSE LES CHIENS FOUS ET LES VACHES MINCES. JE SUIS TRÈS BIZARRE. JE NE SUIS PAS INQUIET. (a female would say INQUIÈTE)

5. J'ENTENDS LA PERCEUSE ET JE VOIS UNE BÊCHE PLEINE

110

## ELEMENTARY GRAMMAR

To use the words HER and HIM in sentences such as I EAT HIM or SEE HER, and so on, then in French the word for HIM is LE, and the word for HER is LA.

The word order for such sentences is:

> I HIM EAT  –  JE LE MANGE
>
> I HER SEE  –  JE LA VOIS

Obviously, LE and LA become L before a vowel. For example,

> I KISS HER is JE L'EMBRASSE

Now cover up the answers below and translate the following:

(You can write your answers in)

1. I WANT THE DOG, AND I AM PUTTING HIM ON THE TABLE

2. I HEAR THE DIRTY GIRL, AND I KISS HER

3. I AM FILLING THE CUP. DO YOU WANT THE COFFEE?

4. I AM HELPING THE STRONG ROPE, BUT I HEAR HIM

5. THE WIRE IS VERY WEAK

The answers are:

1. JE VEUX LE CHIEN, ET JE LE METS SUR LA TABLE

2. J'ENTENDS LA JEUNE FILLE SALE, ET JE L'EMBRASSE

3. JE REMPLIS LA TASSE. EST-CE QUE VOUS VOULEZ LE CAFÉ?

4. J'AIDE LA CORDE FORTE, MAIS JE L'ENTENDS

5. LE FIL EST TRÈS FAIBLE

## PARTS OF THE HOUSE

**THINK OF EACH IMAGE IN YOUR MIND'S EYE FOR ABOUT TEN SECONDS**

○ The French for ATTIC is MANSARDE
Imagine the MOON'S HARD to see in an attic.

○ The French for BASEMENT is SOUS-SOL
Imagine getting SOZZLED in a basement.

○ The French for DOORBELL is SONNETTE
Imagine ringing a door bell which recites a Shakespearian SONNET.

○ The French for (sliding) BOLT is VERROU
Imagine a VERY big bolt.

○ The French for ORCHARD is VERGER
Imagine a VERGER running round an orchard.

○ The French for CORRIDOR is COULOIR
Imagine a COOL WAR fought in a corridor.

○ The French for GATE is BARRIÈRE
Imagine a gate is a BARRIER.

○ The French for RENT is LOYER
Imagine you need a LAWYER to collect your rent.

○ The French for VILLA is VILLA
Imagine a VILLA shaped like the Eiffel Tower.

○ The French for FLAT is APPARTEMENT
Imagine a flat is an APARTMENT.

## YOU CAN WRITE YOUR ANSWERS IN

○ What is the English for APPARTEMENT? _____

○ What is the English for VILLA? _____

○ What is the English for LOYER? _____

○ What is the English for BARRIÈRE? _____

○ What is the English for COULOIR? _____

○ What is the English for VERGER? _____

○ What is the English for VERROU? _____

○ What is the English for SONNETTE? _____

○ What is the English for SOUS-SOL? _____

○ What is the English for MANSARDE? _____

## TURN BACK FOR THE ANSWERS

# GENDERS

## THINK OF EACH IMAGE IN YOUR MIND'S EYE FOR ABOUT TEN SECONDS

○ The gender for ATTIC is FEMININE     LA MANSARDE
Imagine you store old bottles of perfume in your attic.

○ The gender for BASEMENT is MASCULINE     LE SOUS-SOL
Imagine you see a boxing match in a basement.

○ The gender for DOOR BELL is FEMININE     LA SONNETTE
Imagine a bottle of perfume hanging from a door bell.

○ The gender for (sliding) BOLT is MASCULINE     LE VERROU
Imagine you knock out a boxer with a bolt from the blue.

○ The gender for ORCHARD is MASCULINE     LE VERGER
Imagine a boxer lying in an orchard.

○ The gender for CORRIDOR is MASCULINE     LE COULOIR
Imagine a boxing match in a corridor.

○ The gender for GATE is FEMININE     LA BARRIÈRE
Imagine a bottle of perfume on top of a gate.

○ The gender for RENT is MASCULINE     LE LOYER
Imagine a boxer who rents his shorts.

○ The gender for VILLA is FEMININE     LA VILLA
Imagine a beautiful villa smelling of fragrant perfume.

○ The gender for FLAT is MASCULINE     L'APPARTEMENT (m)
Imagine a boxer who owns a huge flat.

# YOU CAN WRITE YOUR ANSWERS IN

○ What is the gender and French for flat?

○ What is the gender and French for villa?

○ What is the gender and French for rent?

○ What is the gender and French for gate?

○ What is the gender and French for corridor?

○ What is the gender and French for orchard?

○ What is the gender and French for bolt?

○ What is the gender and French for door bell?

○ What is the gender and French for basement?

○ What is the gender and French for attic?

## TURN BACK FOR THE ANSWERS

Now cover up the answers below and translate the following:

(You can write your answers in)

1. I SEE THE ATTIC, THE ORCHARD AND THE VILLA

2. HE DOES NOT WANT THE BASEMENT AND SHE DOES NOT SEE THE FLAT

3. THE DOOR BELL IS WONDERFUL AND I AM GOING TO EAT HERE

4. THE RENT IS QUITE STUPID, AND I SAY, 'I AM IN THE CORRIDOR'

5. I AM GOING TO EAT THE BOLT BUT I WANT THE OPEN GATE

The answers are

1. JE VOIS LA MANSARDE, LE VERGER ET LA VILLA

2. IL NE VEUT PAS LE SOUS-SOL ET ELLE NE VOIT PAS L'APPARTEMENT

3. LA SONNETTE EST MERVEILLEUSE ET JE VAIS MANGER ICI. (N.B. MERVEILLEUX, in the feminine is MERVEILLEUSE)

4. LE LOYER EST ASSEZ STUPIDE ET JE DIS, 'JE SUIS DANS LE COULOIR'

5. JE VAIS MANGER LE VERROU MAIS JE VEUX LA BARRIÈRE OUVERTE

## Section 6 BITS AND PIECES, FAMILY WORDS

**THINK OF EACH IMAGE IN YOUR MIND'S EYE FOR ABOUT TEN SECONDS**

○ The French for COMB is PEIGNE
Imagine paying a PENNY for a comb.

○ The French for BRUSH is BROSSE
Imagine seeing a BRUISE where a child has been hit by a brush.

○ The French for BELT is CEINTURE
Imagine a belt round the CENTRE of your tummy.

○ The French for BAG is SAC
Imagine a big SACK being used as a handbag.

○ The French for JEWEL is BIJOU
Imagine asking the queen, 'BE YOU wearing your jewels tonight, queen?'

○ The French for BUTTON IS BOUTON
Imagine you put your BOAT ON a button.

○ The French for CORK is BOUCHON
Imagine a BUSH ON a cork.

○ The French for BOX is BOÎTE
Imagine a little BRAT finding your secret box.

○ The French for PAPER is PAPIER
Imagine dropping paper from the Eiffel Tower.

○ The French for INK is ENCRE
Imagine a ship's ANCHOR covered all over in ink.

Note: Do not confuse this image with INQUIET.

## YOU CAN WRITE YOUR ANSWERS IN

○ What is the English for ENCRE? _____

○ What is the English for PAPIER? _____

○ What is the English for BOÎTE? _____

○ What is the English for BOUCHON? _____

○ What is the English for BOUTON? _____

○ What is the English for BIJOU? _____

○ What is the English for SAC? _____

○ What is the English for CEINTURE? _____

○ What is the English for BROSSE? _____

○ What is the English for PEIGNE? _____

TURN BACK FOR THE ANSWERS

120

## GENDERS

**THINK OF EACH IMAGE IN YOUR MIND'S EYE FOR ABOUT TEN SECONDS**

○ The gender of COMB is MASCULINE      **LE PEIGNE**
Imagine a boxer combing his hair.

○ The gender of BRUSH is FEMININE      **LA BROSSE**
Imagine brushing perfume into your
clothes.

○ The gender of BELT is FEMININE      **LA CEINTURE**
Imagine spraying perfume onto your belt.

○ The gender of BAG is MASCULINE      **LE SAC**
Imagine bundling a boxer into a bag.

○ The gender of JEWEL is MASCULINE      **LE BIJOU**
Imagine a boxer with jewels all over his
boxing trunks.

○ The gender of BUTTON is MASCULINE      **LE BOUTON**
Imagine a boxer with buttons on his
trunks.

○ The gender of CORK is MASCULINE      **LE BOUCHON**
Imagine putting a cork into a boxer's
mouth.

○ The gender of BOX is FEMININE      **LA BOÎTE**
Imagine putting a bottle of perfume in
a box.

○ The gender of PAPER is MASCULINE      **LE PAPIER**
Imagine a boxer stuffing his gloves with
paper.

○ The gender of INK is FEMININE      **L'ENCRE (f)**
Imagine ink in a perfume bottle.

## YOU CAN WRITE YOUR ANSWERS IN

○ What is the gender and French for ink? _____

○ What is the gender and French for paper? _____

○ What is the gender and French for box? _____

○ What is the gender and French for cork? _____

○ What is the gender and French for button? _____

○ What is the gender and French for jewel? _____

○ What is the gender and French for bag? _____

○ What is the gender and French for belt? _____

○ What is the gender and French for brush? _____

○ What is the gender and French for comb? _____

## TURN BACK FOR THE ANSWERS

## SOME USEFUL WORDS

### THINK OF EACH IMAGE IN YOUR MIND'S EYE FOR ABOUT TEN SECONDS

○ The French for LUKEWARM is TIÈDE
Imagine saying to your friend, 'This TEA, ED, is lukewarm.'

○ The French for ENERGETIC is ÉNERGIQUE
Imagine running energetically up the Eiffel Tower.

○ The French for ALSO is AUSSI
Imagine telling a visitor to France, 'OH, SEE the Louvre also.'

○ The French for AGAINST is CONTRE
Imagine someone being against you and CONTRAdicting you all the time.

○ The French for ALMOST is PRESQUE
Imagine someone almost PRESSED you flat.

○ The French for BETWEEN is ENTRE
Imagine someone making an ENTRY between some pillars.

○ The French for ALWAYS is TOUJOURS
Imagine I'm always friendly TO YOUR mother.

○ The French for DURING is PENDANT
Imagine a PENDANT swinging during a performance by a singer.

○ The French for IMMEDIATELY is IMMÉDIATEMENT
Imagine telling someone to go up the Eiffel Tower immediately.

○ The French for HEALTHY is SAIN
Imagine keeping healthy by swimming in the SEINE every day.

# YOU CAN WRITE YOUR ANSWERS IN

○ What is the English for SAIN? _____

○ What is the English for IMMÉDIATEMENT? _____

○ What is the English for PENDANT? _____

○ What is the English for TOUJOURS? _____

○ What is the English for ENTRE? _____

○ What is the English for PRESQUE? _____

○ What is the English for CONTRE? _____

○ What is the English for AUSSI? _____

○ What is the English for ÉNERGIQUE? _____

○ What is the English for TIÈDE? _____

## TURN BACK FOR THE ANSWERS

COVER UP THE LEFT HAND PAGE

○ What is the French for healthy? _____

○ What is the French for immediately? _____

○ What is the French for during? _____

○ What is the French for always? _____

○ What is the French for between? _____

○ What is the French for almost? _____

○ What is the French for against? _____

○ What is the French for also? _____

○ What is the French for energetic? _____

○ What is the French for lukewarm? _____

TURN BACK FOR THE ANSWERS

**Note**
For the words you have just learned:
HEALTHY is SAIN (masculine), SAINE (feminine)

The other words you have just learned are the same in the masculine and in the feminine.

**SOME VERBS**

**THINK OF EACH IMAGE IN YOUR MIND'S EYE FOR ABOUT TEN SECONDS**

○ The French for I BUY is J'ACHÈTE
  Imagine I BUY A SHED for the back yard.

○ The French for I HIRE is JE LOUE
  Imagine I HIRE a LOO for the day.

○ The French for I SCREAM is JE CRIE
  Imagine I CREate a fuss by SCREAMING.

○ The French for I CALL is J'APPELLE
  Imagine you are the kind of person who CALLS an APPLE an apple.

## YOU CAN WRITE YOUR ANSWERS IN

○ What is the English for J'APPELLE? _____

○ What is the English for JE CRIE? _____

○ What is the English for JE LOUE? _____

○ What is the English for J'ACHÈTE? _____

**TURN BACK FOR THE ANSWERS**

## COVER UP THE LEFT HAND SIDE

○ What is the French for I call?   _____

○ What is the French for I scream?   _____

○ What is the French for I hire?   _____

○ What is the French for I buy?   _____

## TURN BACK FOR THE ANSWERS

Now cover up the answers below and translate the following:

(You can write your answers in)

1. I BOUGHT THE COMB AND THE CORK IN A SHOP,
   BUT I AM BUYING THE BELT AND THE JEWELS
   DURING THE NIGHT

2. I HIRED THE LUKEWARM INK, THE PAPER AND THE
   BRUSH

3. THE BLACK BAG IS ALMOST ALWAYS CLOSED

4. I WANT THE CLEAR BUTTONS IMMEDIATELY

5. I LIKE HIM ALSO BETWEEN THE BED AND THE
   CHAIR. I AM VERY HEALTHY!

The answers are:

1. J'AI ACHETÉ LE PEIGNE ET LE BOUCHON DANS UN
   MAGASIN, MAIS J'ACHÈTE LA CEINTURE ET LES
   BIJOUX PENDANT LA NUIT

2. J'AI LOUÉ L'ENCRE TIÈDE, LE PAPIER ET LA
   BROSSE

3. LE SAC NOIR EST PRESQUE TOUJOURS FERMÉ

4. JE VEUX LES BOUTONS CLAIRS IMMÉDIATEMENT

5. JE L'AIME AUSSI ENTRE LE LIT ET LA CHAISE. JE
   SUIS TRÈS SAIN! (A woman would say SAINE)

## ELEMENTARY GRAMMAR

In the last section, you saw that to say sentences such as I SEE HIM, I EAT HER, and so on, you change the word order around so that the sentence becomes I HIM SEE, and so on.

You will remember that in French there are no neuter words. All words are either masculine or feminine. This means that there is effectively no word for IT.

When you want to say, for example, I EAT IT, the 'it' becomes either masculine or feminine – depending on what 'it' stands for.

For example, if you want to say I EAT IT and the 'it' stands for FISH, then in French the sentence is JE LE MANGE, because 'the fish' is LE POISSON.

If you want to say I EAT IT and the 'it' stands for COW, then you say JE LA MANGE, because 'the cow' is LA VACHE.

But remember, this is only for sentences such as I LIKE IT, I EAT IT and so on. For sentences such as IT SEES THE COW, you use IL or ELLE as if it were HE or SHE.

Now cover up the answers below and translate the following:

(You can write your answers in)

1. I AM AGAINST THE RIPE FRUIT, BUT I EAT IT
2. I HIRE THE LAZY DOG
3. I LIKE THE BOX, AND THE HUSBAND LIKES IT ALSO
4. THE WINE IS DELICIOUS AND I PUT IT ON THE CARPET
5. DURING MY JOURNEY, I CALL THE WAITER

The answers are:

1. JE SUIS CONTRE LE FRUIT MÛR, MAIS JE LE MANGE
2. JE LOUE LE CHIEN PARESSEUX
3. J'AIME LA BOÎTE, ET LE MARI L'AIME AUSSI
4. LE VIN EST DÉLICIEUX ET JE LE METS SUR LE TAPIS
5. PENDANT MON VOYAGE, J'APPELLE LE GARÇON

## FAMILY WORDS

## THINK OF EACH IMAGE IN YOUR MIND'S EYE FOR ABOUT TEN SECONDS

○ The French for NIECE is NIÈCE
  Imagine taking your niece to see the Eiffel Tower.

○ The French for PARENTS is PARENTS
  Imagine your parents drag you up the Eiffel Tower.

○ The French for WIDOW is VEUVE
  Imagine a widow with a lot of VERVE.

○ The French for WIDOWER is VEUF
  Imagine a widower without a WIFE.

○ The French for BRIDEGROOM is MARIÉ
  Imagine bridegrooms always MARRY women.

○ The French for ADULT is ADULTE
  Imagine the Eiffel Tower is for adults only.

○ The French for CHILD is ENFANT
  Imagine a child is an INFANT.

○ The French for GRANDFATHER is GRAND'PÈRE
  Imagine your grandfather with a GRAND PAIR of trousers.

○ The French for GRANDMOTHER is GRAND'MÈRE
  Imagine your grandmother riding a GRAND MARE.

○ The French for NEPHEW is NEVEU
  Imagine your nephew is in the NAVY.

# YOU CAN WRITE YOUR ANSWERS IN

○ What is the English for NEVEU? _____

○ What is the English for GRAND'MÈRE? _____

○ What is the English for GRAND'PÈRE? _____

○ What is the English for ENFANT? _____

○ What is the English for ADULTE? _____

○ What is the English for MARIÉ? _____

○ What is the English for VEUF? _____

○ What is the English for VEUVE? _____

○ What is the English for PARENTS? _____

○ What is the English for NIÈCE? _____

## TURN BACK FOR THE ANSWERS

## GENDERS

**THINK OF EACH IMAGE IN YOUR MIND'S EYE FOR ABOUT TEN SECONDS**

○ The gender of NIECE is FEMININE        LA NIÈCE
Imagine giving your niece perfume as
a present.

○ The gender of PARENTS is MASCULINE    LES PARENTS
Imagine your parents are boxing each      (masculine plural)
other.

○ The gender of WIDOW is FEMININE       LA VEUVE
Imagine a young widow who covers herself
in perfume.

○ The gender of WIDOWER is MASCULINE     LE VEUF
Imagine a widower who takes up boxing to
forget his grief.

○ The gender of BRIDEGROOM is        LE MARIÉ
MASCULINE
Imagine the bridegroom is a famous boxer.

○ The gender of ADULT is MASCULINE    L'ADULTE (m or f)
OR FEMININE
Imagine adults can be male or female.

○ The gender of CHILD is MASCULINE     L'ENFANT (m or f)
OR FEMININE
Imagine children can be male or female.

○ The gender of GRANDFATHER is      LE GRAND'PÈRE
MASCULINE
Imagine your grandfather used to be
a boxer.

○ The gender of GRANDMOTHER is     LA GRAND'MÈRE
FEMININE
Imagine your grandmother putting on
lavender water perfume.

○ The gender of NEPHEW is MASCULINE     LE NEVEU
Imagine your nephew training to be a
boxer.

135

## YOU CAN WRITE YOUR ANSWERS IN

○ What is the gender and French for nephew? _____

○ What is the gender and French for grandmother? _____

○ What is the gender and French for grandfather? _____

○ What is the gender and French for child? _____

○ What is the gender and French for adult? _____

○ What is the gender and French for bridegroom? _____

○ What is the gender and French for widower? _____

○ What is the gender and French for widow? _____

○ What is the gender and French for parents? _____

○ What is the gender and French for niece? _____

## TURN BACK FOR THE ANSWERS

Now cover up the answers below and translate the following:

(You can write your answers in)

1. I SCREAM AND I CALL THE NIECE AND THE NEPHEW

2. THE GRANDFATHER IS BETWEEN THE WIDOWER AND THE WIDOW

3. DURING THE WEEK I BUY A BRIDEGROOM BUT NOT A CHILD

4. THE PARENTS OF THE GRANDMOTHER ARE HEALTHY

5. WHEN AN ADULT IS AGAINST THE WALL, HE IS ALWAYS WET

The answers are:

1. JE CRIE ET J'APPELLE LA NIÈCE ET LE NEVEU

2. LE GRAND'PÈRE EST ENTRE LE VEUF ET LA VEUVE

3. PENDANT LA SEMAINE J'ACHÈTE UN MARIÉ MAIS PAS UN ENFANT

4. LES PARENTS DE LA GRAND'MÈRE SONT SAINS

5. QUAND UN ADULTE EST CONTRE LE MUR, IL EST TOUJOURS MOUILLÉ

## Section 7   MISCELLANEOUS USEFUL WORDS, SEASONS

**THINK OF EACH IMAGE IN YOUR MIND'S EYE FOR ABOUT TEN SECONDS**

○ The French for FARMER is FERMIER
   Imagine a farmer is coming FOR ME.

○ The French for FIELD is CHAMP
   Imagine being SHOWN a field.

○ The French for HOLE is TROU
   Imagine asking if it is TRUE that you fell down a hole.

○ The French for LEATHER is CUIR
   Imagine thinking that is QUEER looking leather.

○ The French for CLOTH is ÉTOFFE
   Imagine you ATE OFF some cloth.

○ The French for STAIN is TACHE
   Imagine you DASH out to remove a stain.

○ The French for GUEST is INVITÉ
   Imagine you INVITE a guest to tea.

○ The French for MIDDLE is CENTRE
   Imagine looking at the middle, the CENTRE of a doughnut.

○ The French for END is FIN
   Imagine someone using a FAN at the end of a performance.

○ The French for COAST is CÔTE
   Imagine putting on your COAT as you reach the coast.

   (Remember la côte also means the rib)

## YOU CAN WRITE YOUR ANSWERS IN

○ What is the English for CÔTE? _____

○ What is the English for FIN? _____

○ What is the English for CENTRE? _____

○ What is the English for INVITÉ? _____

○ What is the English for TACHE? _____

○ What is the English for ÉTOFFE? _____

○ What is the English for CUIR? _____

○ What is the English for TROU? _____

○ What is the English for CHAMP? _____

○ What is the English for FERMIER? _____

## TURN BACK FOR THE ANSWERS

## GENDERS

### THINK OF EACH IMAGE IN YOUR MIND'S EYE FOR ABOUT TEN SECONDS

○ The gender of FARMER is MASCULINE       **LE FERMIER**
  Imagine a farmer watching a boxing match.

○ The gender of FIELD is MASCULINE       **LE CHAMP**
  Imagine a boxing match in a field.

○ The gender of HOLE is MASCULINE       **LE TROU**
  Imagine a boxer falling down a hole.

○ The gender of LEATHER is MASCULINE       **LE CUIR**
  Imagine a boxer with leather trunks.

○ The gender of CLOTH is FEMININE       **L'ÉTOFFE (f)**
  Imagine spraying perfume all over a piece
  of cloth.

○ The gender of STAIN is FEMININE       **LA TACHE**
  Imagine spraying perfume to cover a stain.

○ The gender of (male) GUEST is       **L'INVITÉ (m)**
  MASCULINE
  Imagine inviting a boxer home as your
  guest.
  * A female guest is spelt INVITÉE

○ The gender of MIDDLE is MASCULINE       **LE CENTRE**
  Imagine hitting a boxer in his middle.

○ The gender of END is FEMININE       **LA FIN**
  Imagine the end of a bottle of perfume.

○ The gender of COAST is FEMININE       **LA CÔTE**
  Imagine the coast smells of fragrant
  perfume.

## YOU CAN WRITE YOUR ANSWERS IN

○ What is the gender and French for coast? _____

○ What is the gender and French for end? _____

○ What is the gender and French for middle? _____

○ What is the gender and French for guest? _____

○ What is the gender and French for stain? _____

○ What is the gender and French for cloth? _____

○ What is the gender and French for leather? _____

○ What is the gender and French for hole? _____

○ What is the gender and French for field? _____

○ What is the gender and French for farmer? _____

## TURN BACK FOR THE ANSWERS

## SOME USEFUL WORDS

**THINK OF EACH IMAGE IN YOUR MIND'S EYE FOR ABOUT TEN SECONDS**

○ The French for BEFORE (of time) is AVANT
  Imagine saying to someone, 'You'll be in HEAVEN before me.'

○ The French for AFTER is APRÈS
  Imagine I PRAY after every meal.

○ The French for UNHAPPY is MALHEUREUX
  Imagine you MAIL HER an unhappy letter.

○ The French for MANY is BEAUCOUP
  Imagine saying BOO-COW many times.

○ The French for IMPOSSIBLE is IMPOSSIBLE
  Imagine it is impossible to eat the Eiffel Tower.

○ The French for WORSE is PIRE
  Imagine there is nothing worse than a PEER of the Realm.

○ The French for FRESH is FRAIS
  Imagine something is fresh and FREE.

○ The French for POSSIBLE is POSSIBLE
  Imagine it is possible to jump off the Eiffel Tower.

○ The French for QUIET is CALME
  Imagine something is quiet and CALM.

○ The French for FALSE is FAUX
  Imagine your FOE is false.

## YOU CAN WRITE YOUR ANSWERS IN

○ What is the English for FAUX?  _____

○ What is the English for CALME?  _____

○ What is the English for POSSIBLE?  _____

○ What is the English for FRAIS?  _____

○ What is the English for PIRE?  _____

○ What is the English for IMPOSSIBLE?  _____

○ What is the English for BEAUCOUP?  _____

○ What is the English for MALHEUREUX?  _____

○ What is the English for APRÈS?  _____

○ What is the English for AVANT?  _____


## TURN BACK FOR THE ANSWERS

COVER UP THE LEFT HAND PAGE

○ What is the French for false? _____

○ What is the French for quiet? _____

○ What is the French for possible? _____

○ What is the French for fresh? _____

○ What is the French for worse? _____

○ What is the French for impossible? _____

○ What is the French for many? _____

○ What is the French for unhappy? _____

○ What is the French for after? _____

○ What is the French for before? _____

TURN BACK FOR THE ANSWERS

**Note**

1. To say MANY COWS, MANY DOGS, and so on, you must say BEAUCOUP *DE* VACHES, BEAUCOUP *DE* CHIENS, and so on.
2. CALME and TRANQUILLE can both mean QUIET.
3. For the words you have just learned
UNHAPPY is MALHEUREUX (masculine),
MALHEUREUSE (feminine)
FRESH is FRAIS (masculine), FRAÎCHE (feminine)
FALSE is FAUX (masculine), FAUSSE (feminine)
4. Remember that FRAIS or FRAÎCHE also means COOL.

The other words you have just learned are the same in the masculine and in the feminine.

**SOME VERBS**

## THINK OF EACH IMAGE IN YOUR MIND'S EYE FOR ABOUT TEN SECONDS

○ The French for I SMOKE is JE FUME
   Imagine FUMES come from you when you SMOKE.

○ The French for I UNDERSTAND is JE COMPRENDS
   Imagine, 'I COMPREHEND, I UNDERSTAND.'

○ The French for I RUN is JE COURS
   Imagine thinking, 'I can CURE that man of the way he RUNS.'

○ The French for I BRING is J'APPORTE
   Imagine I BRING things in through A PORT.

○ The French for I CARRY is JE PORTE
   Imagine PORTERS CARRYING things.

**YOU CAN WRITE YOUR ANSWERS IN**

○ What is the English for JE PORTE? _____

○ What is the English for J'APPORTE? _____

○ What is the English for JE COURS? _____

○ What is the English for JE COMPRENDS? _____

○ What is the English for JE FUME? _____

**TURN BACK FOR THE ANSWERS**

148

## COVER UP THE LEFT HAND PAGE

○ What is the French for I carry?        _____

○ What is the French for I bring?        _____

○ What is the French for I run?        _____

○ What is the French for I understand?     _____

○ What is the French for I smoke?       _____

**TURN BACK FOR THE ANSWERS**

Now cover up the answers below and translate the following:

(You can write your answers in)

1. I SMOKE IN A QUIET FIELD WITH A FARMER AND A GUEST

2. AFTER MIDNIGHT I RUN IN THE FIRST FIELD

3. THE FRESH HOLE IS IN THE GREY CLOTH

4. I UNDERSTAND THE MIDDLE BUT NOT THE END. THE GUEST IS FALSE

5. I SEE AN IMPOSSIBLE STAIN ON THE FRESH LEATHER

The answers are:

1. JE FUME DANS UN CHAMP CALME AVEC UN FERMIER ET UN INVITÉ

2. APRÈS MINUIT JE COURS DANS LE PREMIER CHAMP

3. LE TROU FRAIS EST DANS L'ÉTOFFE GRISE

4. JE COMPRENDS LE CENTRE MAIS PAS LA FIN. L'INVITÉ EST FAUX

5. JE VOIS UNE TACHE IMPOSSIBLE SUR LE CUIR FRAIS

## ELEMENTARY GRAMMAR

The words for ME, YOU, US and THEM in sentences like HE EATS ME, THE CAT WANTS YOU, and so on, are as follows:

ME – ME

YOU – VOUS

US – NOUS

THEM – LES

The word order works in exactly the same way as you learned with HIM, HER and IT. For example,

HE EATS ME  is  IL ME MANGE

THE DOG EATS YOU  is  LE CHIEN VOUS MANGE

Now cover up the answers below and translate the following:

(You can write your answers in)

1. I CARRY YOU AND HE CARRIES ME

2. I BRING YOU THE CLOTH AND I BRING YOU A LETTER

3. THE COAST IS BETTER THAN THE TOWN BUT WORSE THAN THE MOUNTAINS

4. I SEE MANY FIELDS BUT HE DOES NOT SEE THE FIRST COAST BEFORE TEN O'CLOCK

5. I UNDERSTAND YOU AND I UNDERSTAND THEM

The answers are:

1. JE VOUS PORTE ET IL ME PORTE

2. JE VOUS APPORTE L'ÉTOFFE, ET JE VOUS APPORTE UNE LETTRE

3. LA CÔTE EST MEILLEURE QUE LA VILLE MAIS PIRE QUE LES MONTAGNES

4. JE VOIS BEAUCOUP DE CHAMPS MAIS IL NE VOIT PAS LA PREMIÈRE CÔTE AVANT DIX HEURES

5. JE VOUS COMPRENDS ET JE LES COMPRENDS

# SOME MORE USEFUL WORDS

## THINK OF EACH IMAGE IN YOUR MIND'S EYE FOR ABOUT TEN SECONDS

○ The French for both BIRTHDAY and ANNIVERSARY is ANNIVERSAIRE
Imagine going to visit the Eiffel Tower on your birthday or anniversary.

○ The French for CHRISTMAS is NOËL
Imagine singing the carol, 'The First NOËL' at Christmas time.

○ The French for EASTER is PÂQUES
Imagine you PACK for your Easter holidays.

○ The French for SPRING is PRINTEMPS
Imagine you wished spring would arrive PRONTO.

○ The French for SUMMER is ÉTÉ
Imagine you hope to see EIGHTY summers.

○ The French for AUTUMN is AUTOMNE
Imagine it's HOT ON an autumn day.

○ The French for WINTER is HIVER
Imagine you HEAVE HER into the river on a winter's day.

## YOU CAN WRITE YOUR ANSWERS IN

○ What is the English for HIVER?                  _____

○ What is the English for AUTOMNE?                _____

○ What is the English for ÉTÉ?                    _____

○ What is the English for PRINTEMPS?              _____

○ What is the English for PÂQUES?                 _____

○ What is the English for NOËL?                   _____

○ What is the English for
  ANNIVERSAIRE?                                   _____

## TURN BACK FOR THE ANSWERS

154

## GENDERS

**THINK OF EACH IMAGE IN YOUR MIND'S EYE FOR ABOUT TEN SECONDS**

○ The gender of ANNIVERSARY is     L'ANNIVERSAIRE (m)
   MASCULINE
   Imagine it is the anniversary of a famous
   boxing match.

○ The gender of BIRTHDAY is     L'ANNIVERSAIRE (m)
   MASCULINE
   Imagine it is a boxer's birthday.

○ The gender of CHRISTMAS is MASCULINE     NOËL
   Imagine a Christmas party for boxers.
   (*Note:* 'LE' is never used with NOËL)

○ The gender of EASTER is FEMININE     PÂQUES
   Imagine buying perfume for an Easter
   parade.
   (*Note:* 'LA' is never used with PÂQUES)

○ The gender of SPRING is MASCULINE     LE PRINTEMPS
   Imagine a boxing match in the spring
   sunshine.

○ The gender of SUMMER is MASCULINE     L'ÉTÉ (m)
   Imagine an open-air boxing match in the
   summer.

○ The gender of AUTUMN is MASCULINE     L'AUTOMNE (m)
   Imagine boxers train in autumn.

○ The gender of WINTER is MASCULINE     L'HIVER (m)
   Imagine a boxing match on a cold winter's
   night.

# YOU CAN WRITE YOUR ANSWERS IN

○ What is the gender and French for winter? _____

○ What is the gender and French for autumn? _____

○ What is the gender and French for summer? _____

○ What is the gender and French for spring? _____

○ What is the gender and French for Easter? _____

○ What is the gender and French for Christmas? _____

○ What is the gender and French for birthday? _____

○ What is the gender and French for anniversary? _____

## TURN BACK FOR THE ANSWERS

**HERE ARE TWO ADJECTIVES**

**THINK OF EACH IMAGE IN YOUR MIND'S EYE FOR ABOUT TEN SECONDS**

○ The French for ITALIAN is ITALIEN
  Imagine taking a party of Italians to the Eiffel Tower.

○ The French for ENGLISH is ANGLAIS
  Imagine the English like to walk ON CLAY.

YOU CAN WRITE YOUR ANSWERS IN

○ What is the English for ITALIEN? _____

○ What is the English for ANGLAIS? _____

**TURN BACK FOR THE ANSWERS**

## COVER UP THE LEFT HAND PAGE

○ What is the French for Italian?        _____

○ What is the French for English?       _____

TURN BACK FOR THE ANSWERS

**Note**
For the words you have just learned
ITALIAN is ITALIEN (masculine), ITALIENNE (feminine)
ENGLISH is ANGLAIS (masculine), ANGLAISE (feminine)

Now cover up the answers below and translate the following:

(You can write your answers in)

1. MY ANNIVERSARY? I SEE AN ENGLISH CHILD AT
   CHRISTMAS

2. I WAS UNHAPPY. THE WINTER WAS VERY COLD
   AND SUMMER WAS QUIET

3. I CARRY AN ITALIAN GUEST AT EASTER. BRING A
   SHRUB

4. I UNDERSTAND YOU. THE AUTUMN AND THE
   SPRING ARE RED

5. AFTER MY BIRTHDAY MANY PEOPLE ARE
   IMPOSSIBLE

The answers are:

1. MON ANNIVERSAIRE? JE VOIS UN ENFANT
   ANGLAIS À NOËL

2. J'ÉTAIS MALHEUREUX. L'HIVER ÉTAIT TRÈS
   FROID ET L'ÉTÉ ÉTAIT CALME

3. JE PORTE UN INVITÉ ITALIEN À PÂQUES.
   J'APPORTE UN ARBUSTE

4. JE VOUS COMPRENDS. L'AUTOMNE ET LE
   PRINTEMPS SONT ROUGES

5. APRÈS MON ANNIVERSAIRE BEAUCOUP DE GENS
   SONT IMPOSSIBLES

## ELEMENTARY GRAMMAR

You have already learned that the word for:

ME is ME

YOU is VOUS

and

US is NOUS

When you want to say TO ME, TO YOU and TO US, you use the same words. However, the word for TO HIM, TO HER and TO IT is LUI.

Imagine LOUIS XIV giving presents TO HIM, HER and IT.

So, for example:

I BRING THE ROPE TO HIM is JE LUI APPORTE LA CORDE

Notice that the word LUI comes before the verb.

Similarly,

SHE WRITES THE LETTER TO ME is
ELLE M'ÉCRIT LA LETTRE.

Remember that the French word ME becomes M' when it comes before a vowel.

Now cover up the answers below and translate the following:

(You can write your answers in)

1. HE IS SPEAKING TO HER
2. HE IS BRINGING THE CIDER TO YOU
3. I SAY TO HIM 'I AM EATING'
4. THE DOG IS HERE. I AM BRINGING THE BRUSH
   TO IT
5. HE IS SPEAKING TO US

The answers are:

1. IL LUI PARLE
2. IL VOUS APPORTE LE CIDRE
3. JE LUI DIS 'JE MANGE'
4. LE CHIEN EST ICI. JE LUI APPORTE LA BROSSE
5. IL NOUS PARLE

## HERE ARE SOME 'SENSIBLE' REVISION SENTENCES

Cover up the answers below and translate the following:

(You can write your answers in)

1. I HAVE EATEN THE FRENCH BREAD
2. YOUR GRANDSON WAS CHARMING
3. I AM ALONE AT THE HOTEL
4. THE BRIDE IS HAPPY
5. YOU ARE DANCING

The answers are:

1. J'AI MANGÉ LA BAGUETTE
2. VOTRE PETIT-FILS ÉTAIT CHARMANT
3. JE SUIS SEUL À L'HÔTEL
4. L'ÉPOUSE EST HEUREUSE
5. VOUS DANSEZ

Now cover up the answers below and translate the following:

(You can write your answers in)

1. I FOUND THE MONEY
2. I HELPED THE FAMILY
3. HER BROTHER IS BORING
4. HE WAS AT THE VILLA
5. I HAVE FOUND A SANDWICH

The answers are:

1. J'AI TROUVÉ L'ARGENT
2. J'AI AIDÉ LA FAMILLE
3. SON FRÈRE EST ENNUYEUX
4. IL ÉTAIT À LA VILLA
5. J'AI TROUVÉ UN SANDWICH

## Section 8    CAR PARTS, TRADES AND PROFESSIONS

**THINK OF EACH IMAGE IN YOUR MIND'S EYE FOR
ABOUT TEN SECONDS**

○ The French for WINDSCREEN WIPER is ESSUIE-GLACE
  Imagine HIS WEE GLASS has a windscreen wiper stuck
  in it.

○ The French for VALVE is SOUPAPE
  Imagine you serve SOUP UP through a valve.

○ The French for SPARK PLUG is BOUGIE
  Imagine some BOOZY garage mechanic trying to fit a spark
  plug.

○ The French for SILENCER is SILENCIEUX
  Imagine carrying a silencer up the Eiffel Tower.

○ The French for SEAT is SIÈGE
  Imagine you SIEZE a seat.

○ The French for NUT is ÉCROU
  Imagine an AIR CREW trying to fix nuts into a crashing
  plane.

○ The French for HORN is KLAXON
  Imagine listening to a KLAXON horn.

○ The French for GASKET is JOINT
  Imagine the mechanic fixing your gasket is a bit of a
  Don JUAN.

○ The French for DRIVER is CHAUFFEUR
  Imagine when you are a car driver you dress as a
  CHAUFFEUR.

○ The French for CYLINDER is CYLINDRE
  Imagine dropping cylinders from the top of the Eiffel Tower.

## YOU CAN WRITE YOUR ANSWERS IN

○ What is the English for CYLINDRE? _____

○ What is the English for CHAUFFEUR? _____

○ What is the English for JOINT? _____

○ What is the English for KLAXON? _____

○ What is the English for ÉCROU? _____

○ What is the English for SIÈGE? _____

○ What is the English for SILENCIEUX? _____

○ What is the English for BOUGIE? _____

○ What is the English for SOUPAPE? _____

○ What is the English for ESSUIE-GLACE? _____

## TURN BACK FOR THE ANSWERS

## GENDERS

**THINK OF EACH IMAGE IN YOUR MIND'S EYE FOR ABOUT TEN SECONDS**

○ The gender of WINDSCREEN WIPER is MASCULINE
  Imagine a boxer fitting a windscreen wiper.
  L'ESSUIE-GLACE (m)

○ The gender of VALVE is FEMININE
  Imagine a valve on a perfume spray.
  LA SOUPAPE

○ The gender of SPARK PLUG is FEMININE
  Imagine cleaning a spark plug with perfume.
  LA BOUGIE

○ The gender of SILENCER is MASCULINE
  Imagine a boxer trying to put a silencer on his car.
  LE SILENCIEUX

○ The gender of SEAT is MASCULINE
  Imagine a boxer sitting in a car seat at the ring side.
  LE SIÈGE

○ The gender of ÉCROU is MASCULINE
  Imagine a boxer eating nuts and bolts.
  L'ÉCROU (m)

○ The gender of HORN is MASCULINE
  Imagine a boxer pressing his car horn with his boxing glove.
  LE KLAXON

○ The gender of GASKET is MASCULINE
  Imagine a boxer mending a leaky gasket with his boxing gloves on.
  LE JOINT

○ The gender of DRIVER is MASCULINE
  Imagine a boxer being the driver of a car.
  LE CHAUFFEUR

○ The gender of CYLINDER is MASCULINE
  Imagine a boxer lifting cylinders in order to strengthen his arms.
  LE CYLINDRE

167

## YOU CAN WRITE YOUR ANSWERS IN

○ What is the gender and French for
cylinder? _____

○ What is the gender and French for driver? _____

○ What is the gender and French for gasket? _____

○ What is the gender and French for horn? _____

○ What is the gender and French for nut? _____

○ What is the gender and French for seat? _____

○ What is the gender and French for silencer? _____

○ What is the gender and French for spark
plug? _____

○ What is the gender and French for valve? _____

○ What is the gender and French for
windscreen wiper? _____

## TURN BACK FOR THE ANSWERS

## SOME USEFUL WORDS

## THINK OF EACH IMAGE IN YOUR MIND'S EYE FOR ABOUT TEN SECONDS

○ The French for PERFECT is PARFAIT
  Imagine the Eiffel Tower is a perfect building.

○ The French for WITHOUT is SANS
  Imagine you are without a SONG in your heart.

○ The French for BEHIND is DERRIÈRE
  Imagine hearing the London DERRY AIR coming from behind a prison wall.

○ The French for AMONG is PARMI
  Imagine they BAR ME from being among my friends.

○ The French for BAD is MAUVAIS
  Imagine you watch a bad MOVIE.

○ The French for CERTAIN is CERTAIN
  Imagine you are certain that this is the Eiffel Tower.

○ The French for EACH (every) is CHAQUE
  Imagine each SHACK in a shanty town.

○ The French for EVERYTHING is TOUT
  Imagine thinking everything is TOO much.

○ The French for BITTER is AMER
  Imagine feeling bitter because your girlfriend (or boyfriend) is not feeling AMOROUS.

○ The French for VULGAR is VULGAIRE
  Imagine thinking the Eiffel Tower looks vulgar.

## YOU CAN WRITE YOUR ANSWERS IN

○ What is the English for VULGAIRE? _____

○ What is the English for AMER? _____

○ What is the English for TOUT? _____

○ What is the English for CHAQUE? _____

○ What is the English for CERTAIN? _____

○ What is the English for MAUVAIS? _____

○ What is the English for PARMI? _____

○ What is the English for DERRIÈRE? _____

○ What is the English for SANS? _____

○ What is the English for PARFAIT _____

## TURN BACK FOR THE ANSWERS

## COVER UP THE LEFT HAND PAGE

○ What is the French for vulgar? _____

○ What is the French for bitter? _____

○ What is the French for everything? _____

○ What is the French for each? _____

○ What is the French for certain? _____

○ What is the French for bad? _____

○ What is the French for among? _____

○ What is the French for behind? _____

○ What is the French for without? _____

○ What is the French for perfect? _____

### TURN BACK FOR THE ANSWERS

**Note**
For the words you have just learned

PERFECT is PARFAIT (masculine), PARFAITE (feminine)
BAD is MAUVAIS (masculine), MAUVAISE (feminine)
CERTAIN is CERTAIN (masculine), CERTAINE (feminine)

The other words you have just learned are the same in the masculine and in the feminine.

Now cover up the answers below and translate the following:

(You can write your answers in)

1. THE WINDSCREEN WIPERS ARE VERY BAD

2. THE SEAT WAS ALWAYS FIRM BEHIND THE DRIVER

3. THE WIFE WAS HERE WITHOUT HER VALVES AND
   EVERYTHING WAS VERY QUIET

4. I BOUGHT THE SPARK PLUGS, AND THE DRIVER
   HAS A NEW SILENCER

5. THE CYLINDER IS IN THE TOWN HALL ALSO

The answers are:

1. LES ESSUIE-GLACE SONT TRÈS MAUVAIS

2. LE SIÈGE ÉTAIT TOUJOURS FERME DERRIÈRE
   LE CHAUFFEUR

3. L'ÉPOUSE ÉTAIT ICI SANS SES SOUPAPES ET TOUT
   ÉTAIT TRÈS TRANQUILLE (or CALME)

4. J'AI ACHETÉ LES BOUGIES, ET LE CHAUFFEUR A
   UN NOUVEAU SILENCIEUX

5. LE CYLINDRE EST DANS LA MAIRIE AUSSI

**Note**
The word ESSUIE-GLACE is 'invariable' i.e. it doesn't add an S in
the plural

## ELEMENTARY GRAMMAR

When you want to say 'THIS dog is good' or 'THAT cat is yellow', and so on, then the word for THIS and THAT in French is CE.

> Imagine saying, 'THIS and THAT, SIR'

When THIS or THAT refers to something feminine, then the word in French is CETTE.

> Imagine THIS woman SET a trap.

The word for THESE and THOSE in both the masculine and feminine is CES.

> Imagine I SAY, 'THESE and THOSE'

So,

> THIS DOG IS GOOD  is  CE CHIEN EST BON
>
> THAT TROUT IS GOOD  is  CETTE TRUITE EST BONNE

(remember that the feminine of BON is BONNE)

> THESE TABLES ARE DIRTY  is  CES TABLES SONT SALES

Now cover up the answers below and translate the following:

(You can write your answers in)

1. THIS PERFECT DRIVER IS ALWAYS BAD BUT THAT AUNT HAS A BETTER CAR

2. THESE GASKETS ARE NEW ALSO. BUT THOSE VALVES ARE NOT NEW

3. THIS HORN IS VERY VULGAR BUT EACH HORN IS VULGAR. I AM CERTAINLY GOING TO EAT

4. THAT BITTER GASKET IS AMONG THE WINDSCREEN WIPERS. I AM PUTTING IT ON THE SEAT

5. THOSE SPARK PLUGS ARE BLACK BUT THIS VALVE AND THESE NUTS ARE WHITE

The answers are

1. CE CHAUFFEUR PARFAIT EST TOUJOURS MAUVAIS MAIS CETTE TANTE A UNE MEILLEURE AUTO (N.B. Note MEILLEUR comes before the noun)

2. CES JOINTS SONT NOUVEAUX AUSSI, MAIS CES SOUPAPES NE SONT PAS NOUVELLES N.B. NOUVEAU takes an 'X' in the masculine plural)

3. CE KLAXON EST TRÈS VULGAIRE MAIS CHAQUE KLAXON EST VULGAIRE. JE VAIS CERTAINEMENT MANGER (N.B. Note the word order)

4. CE JOINT AMER EST PARMI LES ESSUIE-GLACE. JE LE METS SUR LE SIÈGE

5. CES BOUGIES SONT NOIRES MAIS CETTE SOUPAPE ET CES ÉCROUS SONT BLANCS

174

# TRADES AND PROFESSIONS

## THINK OF EACH IMAGE IN YOUR MIND'S EYE FOR ABOUT TEN SECONDS

○ The French for CARPENTER is MENUISIER
Imagine MEN SWEAR AT you if you are a carpenter.

○ The French for PLUMBER is PLOMBIER
Imagine plumbers PLAN B.A. (British Airways) air flights.

○ The French for ARCHITECT is ARCHITECTE
Imagine the architect who designed the Eiffel Tower.

○ The French for BAKER is BOULANGER
Imagine a BULL ON JADED bakers perks them up a bit.

○ The French for BUTCHER is BOUCHER
Imagine a butcher with a BUSHY beard.

○ The French for COOK is CHEF
Imagine a cook is a CHEF.

○ The French for ELECTRICIAN is ÉLECTRICIEN
Imagine electricians wiring the Eiffel Tower.

○ The French for FIREMAN is POMPIER
Imagine POMPOUS firemen.

○ The French for GARDENER is JARDINIER
Imagine gardeners being JARRED IN A sore spot.

○ The French for NURSE is INFIRMIÈRE
Imagine you should respect doctors AND FEAR MERE nurses.

## YOU CAN WRITE YOUR ANSWERS IN

○ What is the English for INFIRMIÈRE     _____

○ What is the English for JARDINIER     _____

○ What is the English for POMPIER     _____

○ What is the English for ÉLECTRICIEN     _____

○ What is the English for CHEF     _____

○ What is the English for BOUCHER     _____

○ What is the English for BOULANGER     _____

○ What is the English for ARCHITECTE     _____

○ What is the English for PLOMBIER     _____

○ What is the English for MENUISIER     _____

## TURN BACK FOR THE ANSWERS

## GENDERS

### THINK OF EACH IMAGE IN YOUR MIND'S EYE FOR ABOUT TEN SECONDS

○ The gender for CARPENTER is         LE MENUISIER
MASCULINE
Imagine a carpenter making a boxing ring.

○ The gender for PLUMBER is         LE PLOMBIER
MASCULINE
Imagine a plumber hitting a boxer with a
lead pipe.

○ The gender for ARCHITECT is     L'ARCHITECTE (m)
MASCULINE
Imagine an architect designing a boxing
arena.

○ The gender for BAKER is MASCULINE    LE BOULANGER
Imagine a baker making a cake in the shape
of a boxing ring.

○ The gender for BUTCHER is         LE BOUCHER
MASCULINE
Imagine a boxer being a real butcher.

○ The gender for COOK is MASCULINE       LE CHEF
Imagine a cook cooking a meal for a boxer.

○ The gender for ELECTRICIAN is    L'ÉLECTRICIEN (m)
MASCULINE
Imagine an electrician electrocuting a boxer
by mistake.

○ The gender for FIREMAN is         LE POMPIER
MASCULINE
Imagine a fireman hosing down a boxer.

○ The gender for GARDENER is      LE JARDINIER
MASCULINE
Imagine a gardener fighting a boxer.

○ The gender for NURSE is FEMININE    L'INFIRMIÈRE (f)
Imagine a nurse giving a bottle of perfume
to a patient.

## YOU CAN WRITE YOUR ANSWERS IN

O What is the gender and French for nurse _____

O What is the gender and French for gardener _____

O What is the gender and French for fireman _____

O What is the gender and French for electrician _____

O What is the gender and French for cook _____

O What is the gender and French for butcher _____

O What is the gender and French for baker _____

O What is the gender and French for architect _____

O What is the gender and French for plumber _____

O What is the gender and French for carpenter _____

## TURN BACK FOR THE ANSWERS

Now cover up the answers below and translate the following:

(You can write your answers in)

1. THIS CARPENTER AND THIS COOK ARE BEHIND THE BUTCHER
2. THESE GARDENERS AND THESE NURSES ARE VERY VULGAR
3. EACH FIREMAN HAS A PERFECT ARCHITECT
4. THE ELECTRICIAN IS AMONG THESE PLUMBERS
5. THAT UNHAPPY BAKER WANTS EVERYTHING

The answers are:

1. CE MENUISIER ET CE CHEF SONT DERRIÈRE LE BOUCHER
2. CES JARDINIERS ET CES INFIRMIÈRES SONT TRÈS VULGAIRES
3. CHAQUE POMPIER A UN ARCHITECTE PARFAIT
4. L'ÉLECTRICIEN EST PARMI CES PLOMBIERS
5. CE MALHEUREUX BOULANGER VEUT TOUT

## ELEMENTARY GRAMMAR POINT

You will have noticed that when you say I ATE or I HAVE EATEN in French, you are actually saying I HAVE EATEN – J'AI (I have) MANGÉ (eaten).

In the same way, you can change I HAVE to YOU HAVE (VOUS AVEZ) or HE HAS (IL A) or SHE HAS (ELLE A).
So,

YOU HAVE EATEN or YOU ATE   is   VOUS AVEZ MANGÉ

HE HAS EATEN or HE ATE   is   IL A MANGÉ

SHE HAS EATEN or SHE ATE   is   ELLE A MANGÉE

YOU WROTE   is   VOUS AVEZ ÉCRIT

SHE SPOKE   is   ELLE A PARLÉE

HE HAS WRITTEN   is   IL A ÉCRIT

**Note**
In this course we have used the word 'VOUS' for 'YOU'. There is another word for you – TU. This is used when communicating to a friend or someone you know well. At this stage of learning French you are safer sticking to the 'VOUS' form.

Now cover up the answers below and translate the following:

(You can write your answers in)

1. YOU HAVE CAUGHT THE SEAGULL
2. SHE ATE THE SANDWICH
3. HE HAS FOUND A PANCAKE
4. YOU DANCED ON THE MOTORWAY
5. SHE SPOKE TO THE AUNT

The answers are:

1. VOUS AVEZ ATTRAPPE LA MOUETTE
2. ELLE A MANGÉE LE SANDWICH
3. IL A TROUVÉ UNE CRÊPE
4. VOUS AVEZ DANSÉ SUR L'AUTOROUTE
5. ELLE A PARLÉE À LA TANTE

182

## Section 9   MISCELLANEOUS USEFUL WORDS, PARTS OF THE BODY, TRAVELLING

**THINK OF EACH IMAGE IN YOUR MIND'S EYE FOR ABOUT TEN SECONDS**

○ The French for AIR-CONDITIONING is CLIMATISATION
Imagine you need ACCLIMATISING to the air-conditioning.

○ The French for BAY is BAIE
Imagine you are looking at a bay from the top of the Eiffel Tower.

○ The French for BALCONY is BALCON
Imagine standing on a balcony at the top of the Eiffel Tower.

○ The French for BIBLE is BIBLE
Imagine throwing bibles from the Eiffel Tower.

○ The French for BOARDING HOUSE is PENSION
Imagine spending your old age PENSION on a boarding house.

○ The French for BOTTLE is BOUTEILLE
Imagine sticking bottles on baby's feet instead of BOOTEES.

○ The French for CAR PARK is PARKING
Imagine finding a car PARKING in a car park.

○ The French for CARAVAN is CARAVANE
Imagine driving your caravan under the Eiffel Tower.

○ The French for CASINO is CASINO
Imagine a casino in the Eiffel Tower.

○ The French for CASTLE is CHÂTEAU
Imagine you SHATTER your toe on a castle wall.

## YOU CAN WRITE YOUR ANSWERS IN

○ What is the English for CHÂTEAU? _____

○ What is the English for CASINO? _____

○ What is the English for CARAVANE? _____

○ What is the English for PARKING? _____

○ What is the English for BOUTEILLE? _____

○ What is the English for PENSION? _____

○ What is the English for BIBLE? _____

○ What is the English for BALCON? _____

○ What is the English for BAIE? _____

○ What is the English for
CLIMATISATION? _____

## TURN BACK FOR THE ANSWERS

## GENDERS

**THINK OF EACH IMAGE IN YOUR MIND'S EYE FOR ABOUT TEN SECONDS**

○ The gender of AIR-CONDITIONING   LA CLIMATISATION
  is FEMININE
  Imagine spraying perfume to help the
  air-conditioning.

○ The gender of BAY is FEMININE                    LA BAIE
  Imagine a bay smelling of sweet perfume.

○ The gender of BALCONY is MASCULINE       LE BALCON
  Imagine a boxer falling over a balcony.

○ The gender of BIBLE is FEMININE                 LA BIBLE
  Imagine spilling a bottle of perfume over
  a bible.

○ The gender of BOARDING HOUSE is          LA PENSION
  FEMININE
  Imagine a boarding house which always
  smells of perfume.

○ The gender of BOTTLE is FEMININE       LA BOUTEILLE
  Imagine a bottle of perfume.

○ The gender of CAR PARK is MASCULINE       LE PARKING
  Imagine a boxer parking his car in a
  car park.

○ The gender of CARAVAN is FEMININE    LA CARAVANE
  Imagine spraying the inside of your
  caravan with perfume

○ The gender of CASINO is MASCULINE           LE CASINO
  Imagine boxers gambling in a casino.

○ The gender of CASTLE is MASCULINE      LE CHÂTEAU
  Imagine boxers fighting in a castle.

# YOU CAN WRITE YOUR ANSWERS IN

○ What is the gender and French for castle? _____

○ What is the gender and French for casino? _____

○ What is the gender and French for caravan? _____

○ What is the gender and French for car park? _____

○ What is the gender and French for bottle? _____

○ What is the gender and French for boarding house? _____

○ What is the gender and French for bible? _____

○ What is the gender and French for balcony? _____

○ What is the gender and French for bay? _____

○ What is the gender and French for air-conditioning? _____

## TURN BACK FOR THE ANSWERS

Now cover up answers below and translate the following:

(You can write your answers in)

1. I HEAR THE NEW AIR-CONDITIONING AND THE DISTANT DOOR BELL

2. I AM BRINGING THE SMOOTH BENCH. I LIKE IT IN THE GARDEN

3. THE CASTLE AND THE CASINO ARE VERY VULGAR, BUT THE CAR PARK IS FULL AND THE BOARDING HOUSE IS FORBIDDEN

4. THE BOY IS A TRUE BROTHER, BUT HE IS STRANGE ALSO

5. THE CLEAR BOTTLE IS IN THE QUIET BAY

The answers are:

1. J'ENTENDS LA NOUVELLE CLIMATISATION ET LA SONNETTE LOINTAINE

2. J'APPORTE LE BANC LISSE. JE L'AIME DANS LE JARDIN

3. LE CHÂTEAU ET LE CASINO SONT TRÈS VULGAIRES, MAIS LE PARKING EST PLEIN, ET LA PENSION EST INTERDITE

4. LE GARÇON EST UN VRAI FRÈRE MAIS IL EST BIZARRE AUSSI (N.B. VRAI comes before the word it goes with, with a few exceptions)

5. LA BOUTEILLE CLAIRE EST DANS LA BAIE TRANQUILLE (or CALME)

187

## ELEMENTARY GRAMMAR

You have learned how to say I ASK (JE DEMANDE), I BRING (J'APPORTE) and so on.

It is now very easy, knowing what you know, to say YOU ASK, YOU BRING, and HE or SHE ASKS or BRINGS and so on.

For YOU, all you do is add an AY sound to the end of the 'I' form of the verb, as you saw earlier with YOU EAT – VOUS MANGEZ. The ending is spelled EZ, but pronounced AY.

So,

I ASK  is  JE DEMANDE

YOU ASK  is  VOUS DEMANDEZ

I DANCE  is  JE DANSE

YOU DANCE  is  VOUS DANSEZ

For HE and SHE, you simply use exactly the same form as for 'I'.

So,

I ASK  is  JE DEMANDE

HE or SHE ASKS  is  IL or ELLE DEMANDE

I CARRY  is  JE PORTE

HE or SHE CARRIES  is  IL or ELLE PORTE

Of course, HE or SHE can be replaced by anything HE or SHE can stand for. For example, the form of the verb in the sentence THE DOG DANCES is the same as or HE DANCES. Here are a couple of examples:

HE DANCES  is  IL DANSE

THE DOG DANCES  is  LE CHIEN DANSE

SHE BRINGS  is  ELLE APPORTE

THE COW BRINGS  is  LA VACHE APPORTE

There are some exceptions to this rule which are beyond the scope of this basic course. However, in the sentences you will be asked to translate, we have chosen examples which fit in with the rule. If you make a mistake by using a verb which does not fit in with the rule, you will usually be understood.

Now cover up the answers below and translate the following:

(You can write your answers in)

1. YOU ASK THE UNCLE
2. SHE CARRIES THE CIDER
3. HE CATCHES A HAMMER
4. THE UNCLE SHOWS THE GRANDSON TO THE MOTHER
5. THE DOG FINDS THE CAT

The answers are:

1. VOUS DEMANDEZ À L'ONCLE
2. ELLE PORTE LE CIDRE
3. IL ATTRAPPE UN MARTEAU
4. L'ONCLE MONTRE LE PETIT FILS À LA MÈRE
5. LE CHIEN TROUVE LE CHAT

## SOME MORE USEFUL WORDS

## THINK OF EACH IMAGE IN YOUR MIND'S EYE FOR ABOUT TEN SECONDS

○ The French for CAVE is GROTTE
Imagine a GROTTO in a cave.

○ The French for LOCK is SERRURE
Imagine saying, 'SIR, OUR lock is jammed.'

○ The French for ALARM CLOCK is RÉVEIL
Imagine throwing an alarm clock in the RIVER.

○ The French for CROWD is FOULE
Imagine seeing someone behaving like a FOOL in a large crowd.

○ The French for (a) CUT is COUPURE
Imagine you cut yourself on a COPPER wire.

○ The French for DETOUR is DÉVIATION
Imagine having to make a DEVIATION, a detour.

○ The French for DIET is RÉGIME
Imagine your diet involves a strict REGIME.

○ The French for DITCH is FOSSÉ
Imagine shouting at your wife, 'You silly FOSSIL, we're in the ditch.'

○ The French for ELECTRICITY is ÉLECTRICITÉ
Imagine filling the Eiffel Tower with electricity and shocking all the visitors.

○ The French for EXHIBITION is EXPOSITION
Imagine an EXPOSITION of martial arts at a Chinese exhibition.

## YOU CAN WRITE YOUR ANSWERS IN

○ What is the English for EXPOSITION? _____

○ What is the English for ÉLECTRICITÉ? _____

○ What is the English for FOSSÉ? _____

○ What is the English for RÉGIME? _____

○ What is the English for DÉVIATION? _____

○ What is the English for COUPURE? _____

○ What is the English for FOULE? _____

○ What is the English for RÉVEIL? _____

○ What is the English for SERRURE? _____

○ What is the English for GROTTE? _____

TURN BACK FOR THE ANSWERS

192

# GENDERS

## THINK OF EACH IMAGE IN YOUR MIND'S EYE FOR ABOUT TEN SECONDS

○ The gender of CAVE is FEMININE      LA GROTTE
Imagine finding old bottles of perfume in
a cave.

○ The gender of LOCK is FEMININE      LA SERRURE
Imagine throwing bottles of perfume at a
door lock.

○ The gender of ALARM (CLOCK) is      LE RÉVEIL
MASCULINE
Imagine a boxer awoken by an alarm clock.

○ The gender of CROWD is FEMININE      LA FOULE
Imagine throwing bottles of perfume to a
large crowd.

○ The gender of CUT is FEMININE      LA COUPURE
Imagine pouring perfume into a cut as a
disinfectant.

○ The gender of DEVIATION is      LA DÉVIATION
FEMININE
Imagine spraying perfume on a detour sign.

○ The gender of DIET is MASCULINE      LE RÉGIME
Imagine putting a boxer on a strict diet for
a fight.

○ The gender of DITCH is MASCULINE      LE FOSSÉ
Imagine a boxer falling into a ditch.

○ The gender of ELECTRICITY      L'ÉLECTRICITÉ (f)
is FEMININE
Imagine causing a short circuit by spilling
perfume on a live wire.

○ The gender of EXHIBITION      L'EXPOSITION (f)
is FEMININE
Imagine an exhibition of different
perfumes.

## YOU CAN WRITE YOUR ANSWERS IN

○ What is the gender and French for exhibition? _____

○ What is the gender and French for electricity? _____

○ What is the gender and French for ditch? _____

○ What is the gender and French for diet? _____

○ What is the gender and French for detour? _____

○ What is the gender and French for cut? _____

○ What is the gender and French for crowd? _____

○ What is the gender and French for alarm clock? _____

○ What is the gender and French for lock? _____

○ What is the gender and French for cave? _____

## TURN BACK FOR THE ANSWERS

Now cover up the answers below and translate the following:

(You can write your answers in)

1. MY UNCLE'S CAVE IS DRY, BUT MY AUNT'S LOCK IS WHITE

2. I ASK MY AUNT. SHE ANSWERS MY UNCLE, AND I SEE THE DETOUR

3. I AM SITTING ON THE CHAIR AT THE EXHIBITION, AND I AM READING A WONDERFUL BOOK IN THE CORRIDOR

4. THE CARAVAN IS IN A DITCH AND A CROWD SEES US. YOU HAVE THE ELECTRICITY

5. THE GRANDSON HAS A SERIOUS CUT IN HIS TROUSERS AND HIS DIET IS VERɤ BAD

The answers are:

1. LA GROTTE DE MON ONCLE EST SÈCHE, MAIS LA SERRURE DE MA TANTE EST BLANCHE
2. JE DEMANDE À MA TANTE. ELLE RÉPOND À MON ONCLE, ET JE VOIS LA DÉVIATION
3. JE SUIS ASSIS SUR LA CHAISE À L'EXPOSITION, ET JE LIS UN LIVRE MERVEILLEUX DANS LE COULOIR (a woman would say ASSISE)
4. LA CARAVANE EST DANS UN FOSSÉ ET UNE FOULE NOUS VOIT. VOUS AVEZ L'ÉLECTRICITÉ
5. LE PETIT-FILS A UNE COUPURE GRAVE DANS SON PANTALON ET SON RÉGIME EST TRÈS MAUVAIS

# SOME MORE PARTS OF THE BODY

**THINK OF EACH IMAGE IN YOUR MIND'S EYE FOR ABOUT TEN SECONDS**

○ The French for FACE is VISAGE
Imagine your face is stamped on your VISA.

○ The French for THUMB is POUCE
Imagine your PUSS has thumbs instead of claws.

○ The French for THIGH is CUISSE
Imagine you go all QUEASY when you see a nice thigh.

○ The French for LIP is LÈVRE
Imagine putting a LIVER to your lip to ease a swelling.

○ The French for EAR is OREILLE
Imagine it looks as if a LORRY has run over your ear.

○ The French for VEIN is VEINE
Imagine someone telling you, 'VEN you bite a vein, it bleeds very much.'

○ The French for TEMPLE is TEMPE
Imagine you TAP your temple.

○ The French for SKIN is PEAU
Imagine you POUR something on your skin.

○ The French for KNEE is GENOU
Imagine a Scotsman threatens to feel your knee 'THE NOO'.

○ The French for HEEL is TALON
Imagine an eagle's TALON growing from your heel.

## YOU CAN WRITE YOUR ANSWERS IN

○ What is the English for TALON?  _____

○ What is the English for GENOU?  _____

○ What is the English for PEAU?  _____

○ What is the English for TEMPE?  _____

○ What is the English for VEINE?  _____

○ What is the English for OREILLE?  _____

○ What is the English for LÈVRE?  _____

○ What is the English for CUISSE?  _____

○ What is the English for POUCE?  _____

○ What is the English for VISAGE?  _____

TURN BACK FOR THE ANSWERS

## GENDERS

### THINK OF EACH IMAGE IN YOUR MIND'S EYE FOR ABOUT TEN SECONDS

○ The gender of FACE is MASCULINE
Imagine a boxer's face all spattered with
blood.                                                    LE VISAGE

○ The gender of THUMB is MASCULINE
Imagine a boxer's thumb sticking out of
his glove.                                               LE POUCE

○ The gender of THIGH is FEMININE
Imagine spraying your thigh with perfume.   LA CUISSE

○ The gender of LIP is FEMININE
Imagine spreading perfume over your
sore lips.                                             LA LÈVRE

○ The gender of EAR is FEMININE
Imagine spraying perfume into your ear.    L'OREILLE (f)

○ The gender of VEIN is FEMININE
Imagine perfume instead of blood flows
from your veins.                                       LA VEINE

○ The gender of TEMPLE is FEMININE
Imagine wiping perfume over your temple.   LA TEMPE

○ The gender of SKIN is FEMININE
Imagine you bathe your skin in perfume.     LA PEAU

○ The gender of KNEE is MASCULINE
Imagine a boxer hitting you with his knee.  LE GENOU

○ The gender of HEEL is MASCULINE
Imagine a boxer falling back on his heels.   LE TALON

## YOU CAN WRITE YOUR ANSWERS IN

○ What is the gender and French for heel? _____

○ What is the gender and French for knee? _____

○ What is the gender and French for skin? _____

○ What is the gender and French for temple? _____

○ What is the gender and French for vein? _____

○ What is the gender and French for ear? _____

○ What is the gender and French for lip? _____

○ What is the gender and French for thigh? _____

○ What is the gender and French for thumb? _____

○ What is the gender and French for face? _____

TURN BACK FOR THE ANSWERS

Now cover up the answers below and translate the following:

(You can write your answers in)

1. THE FACE IS FIRMER THAN THE GREEN THUMB, BUT FLATTER THAN AN EAR

2. THE LIPS ARE VERY RED, AND THE THIGHS ARE VERY WEAK

3. I AM CARRYING HER SKIN AND HER KNEE. HER ILLNESS IS WORSE

4. I AM PUTTING HIS HEEL ON THE CLOTH AFTER THE DINNER

5. HIS SMALL TEMPLE IS PALE AND WEAK

The answers are:

1. LE VISAGE EST PLUS FERME QUE LE POUCE VERT, MAIS PLUS PLAT QU'UNE OREILLE (N.B. QUE before a vowel, becomes QU')

2. LES LÈVRES SONT TRÈS ROUGES, ET LES CUISSES SONT TRÈS FAIBLES

3. JE PORTE SA PEAU ET SON GENOU. SA MALADIE EST PIRE

4. JE METS SON TALON SUR L'ÉTOFFE APRÈS LE DÎNER.

5. SA PETITE TEMPE EST PÂLE ET FAIBLE

201

## SOME MORE USEFUL WORDS

### THINK OF EACH IMAGE IN YOUR MIND'S EYE FOR ABOUT TEN SECONDS

○ The French for MATHS is MATHÉMATIQUES
  Imagine doing maths to work out the size of the Eiffel Tower.

○ The French for PHYSICS is PHYSIQUE
  Imagine a knowledge of the physics of materials is necessary to build an Eiffel Tower.

○ The French for CHEMISTRY is CHIMIE
  Imagine a chemistry set SHIMMERING in the sunshine.

○ The French for BIOLOGY is BIOLOGIE
  Imagine a biology lesson at the top of the Eiffel Tower.

○ The French for VELVET is VELOURS
  Imagine velvet on the FLOOR.

○ The French for SLEEVE is MANCHE
  Imagine you watch a moth MUNCH your sleeve.

○ The French for HANDKERCHIEF is MOUCHOIR
  Imagine that if your MOOSH WERE dry, you wouldn't need a handkerchief.

○ The French for SILK is SOIE
  Imagine you look very SUAVE in silk.

○ The French for WOOL is LAINE
  Imagine you LEND your friend a woollen jumper.

○ The French for COTTON is COTON
  Imagine wearing only a cotton dress on top of the Eiffel Tower.

## YOU CAN WRITE YOUR ANSWERS IN

○ What is the English for
  MATHÉMATIQUES? _____

○ What is the English for PHYSIQUE? _____

○ What is the English for CHIMIE? _____

○ What is the English for BIOLOGIE? _____

○ What is the English for VELOURS? _____

○ What is the English for MANCHE? _____

○ What is the English for MOUCHOIR? _____

○ What is the English for SOIE? _____

○ What is the English for LAINE? _____

○ What is the English for COTON? _____

## GENDER

**THINK OF EACH IMAGE IN YOUR MIND'S EYE FOR ABOUT TEN SECONDS**

○ The gender of MATHS is FEMININE plural
Imagine using maths to work out the profit on each bottle of perfume.

LES MATHÉMATIQUES (feminine plural)

○ The gender of PHYSICS is FEMININE
Imagine you need physics to design perfume bottles.

LA PHYSIQUE

○ The gender of CHEMISTRY is FEMININE
Imagine chemistry is what makes a perfume smell.

LA CHIMIE

○ The gender of BIOLOGY is FEMININE
Imagine your biology mistress always smells of perfume.

LA BIOLOGIE

○ The gender of VELVET is MASCULINE
Imagine a boxer with velvet trunks.

LE VELOURS

○ The gender of SLEEVE is FEMININE
Imagine spilling perfume on your sleeve.

LA MANCHE

○ The gender of HANDKERCHIEF is MASCULINE
Imagine a boxer crying into his handkerchief.

LE MOUCHOIR

○ The gender of SILK is FEMININE
Imagine sprinkling good perfume on a silk cloth.

LA SOIE

○ The gender of WOOL is FEMININE
Imagine a bottle of perfume wrapped in a ball of wool.

LA LAINE

○ The gender of COTTON is MASCULINE
Imagine a boxer in cotton underpants.

LE COTON

## YOU CAN WRITE YOUR ANSWERS IN

○ What is the gender and French for
   cotton?                                    _____

○ What is the gender and French for wool?     _____

○ What is the gender and French for silk?     _____

○ What is the gender and French for
   handkerchief?                              _____

○ What is the gender and French for
   sleeve?                                    _____

○ What is the gender and French for
   velvet?                                    _____

○ What is the gender and French for
   biology?                                   _____

○ What is the gender and French for
   chemistry?                                 _____

○ What is the gender and French for
   physics?                                   _____

○ What is the gender and French for
   maths?                                     _____

### TURN BACK FOR THE ANSWERS

**Note**
When talking about mathematics, chemistry and other school sub-
jects you should always put the word for THE in front: LES
MATHÉMATIQUES, LA PHYSIQUE, etc.

Now cover up the answers below and translate the following:

(You can write your answers in)

1. I LIKE MATHS, BUT PHYSICS IS DIFFICULT

2. IS CHEMISTRY BORING? NO, BUT BIOLOGY IS VULGAR

3. MY SLEEVE AND HIS SILK WERE ON THE TABLE

4. WHERE IS THE GREY VELVET? I SEE IT HERE

5. THE HANDKERCHIEF IS GREEN BUT THE WOOL AND THE COTTON ARE BITTER

The answers are:

1. J'AIME LES MATHÉMATIQUES, MAIS LA PHYSIQUE EST DIFFICILE

2. EST-CE QUE LA CHIMIE EST ENNUYEUSE? NON, MAIS LA BIOLOGIE EST VULGAIRE

3. MA MANCHE ET SA SOIE ÉTAIENT SUR LA TABLE

4. OÙ EST LE VELOURS GRIS? JE LE VOIS ICI

5. LE MOUCHOIR EST VERT MAIS LA LAINE ET LE COTON SONT AMERS

## Section 10   MISCELLANEOUS WORDS, CAMPING

**THINK OF EACH IMAGE IN YOUR MIND'S EYE FOR ABOUT TEN SECONDS**

○ The French for FOUNTAIN is FONTAINE
Imagine a fountain under the Eiffel Tower.

○ The French for GIFT is CADEAU
Imagine giving someone a CUDDLE after being given a gift.

○ The French for GUIDE is GUIDE
Imagine a guide noted for his GREED.

○ The French for ISLAND is ÎLE
Imagine EELS covering an island.

○ The French for MOON is LUNE
Imagine a LUNAtic looking at the moon.

○ The French for NAPPY is COUCHE
Imagine a CUSHION over a dirty nappy.

○ The French for NORTH is NORD
Imagine the Eiffel Tower is due north.

○ The French for SOUTH is SUD
Imagine being SUED for driving south.

○ The French for EAST is EST
Imagine looking to the east lEST you miss the sun rising.

○ The French for WEST is OUEST
Imagine the Eiffel Tower is in the west, with the sun setting behind it.

# YOU CAN WRITE YOUR ANSWERS IN

○ What is the English for OUEST?  _____

○ What is the English for EST?  _____

○ What is the English for SUD?  _____

○ What is the English for NORD?  _____

○ What is the English for COUCHE?  _____

○ What is the English for LUNE?  _____

○ What is the English for ÎLE?  _____

○ What is the English for GUIDE?  _____

○ What is the English for CADEAU?  _____

○ What is the English for FONTAINE?  _____

## TURN BACK FOR THE ANSWERS

210

## GENDERS

**THINK OF EACH IMAGE IN YOUR MIND'S EYE FOR ABOUT TEN SECONDS**

○ The gender of FOUNTAIN is FEMININE     LA FONTAINE
Imagine a fountain spurting perfume.

○ The gender of GIFT is MASCULINE     LE CADEAU
Imagine a boxer giving his opponent a gift after a fight.

○ The gender of GUIDE is MASCULINE     LE GUIDE
Imagine a guide taking a group of boxers round.

○ The gender of ISLAND is FEMININE     L'ÎLE (f)
Imagine spraying perfume all over a small island.

○ The gender of MOON is FEMININE     LA LUNE
Imagine astronauts putting a bottle of perfume on the moon.

○ The gender of NAPPY is FEMININE     LA COUCHE
Imagine spraying perfume on a dirty nappy.

○ The gender of NORTH is MASCULINE     LE NORD
Imagine boxers gathering from the north.

○ The gender of SOUTH is MASCULINE     LE SUD
Imagine boxers gathering from the south.

○ The gender of EAST is MASCULINE     L'EST (m)
Imagine boxers gathering from the east.

○ The gender of WEST is MASCULINE     L'OUEST (m)
Imagine boxers gathering from the west.

## YOU CAN WRITE YOUR ANSWERS IN

○ What is the gender and French for west? _____

○ What is the gender and French for east? _____

○ What is the gender and French for south? _____

○ What is the gender and French for North? _____

○ What is the gender and French for nappy? _____

○ What is the gender and French for moon? _____

○ What is the gender and French for island? _____

○ What is the gender and French for guide? _____

○ What is the gender and French for gift? _____

○ What is the gender and French for
fountain? _____

## TURN BACK FOR THE ANSWERS

## ELEMENTARY GRAMMAR

The French for WE is NOUS

> Imagine WE are NEW

The form of the verb is usually got from taking the 'I' form, and adding – ONS.

So,

> I CARRY is JE PORTE
>
> WE CARRY is NOUS PORTONS
>
> I DANCE is JE DANSE
>
> WE DANCE is NOUS DANSONS

There are a number of exceptions to this rule; but as before, in the sentences you have to translate, we have chosen examples which fit in with it. And again, for the most part, you will be understood if you use a verb incorrectly – i.e. that doesn't fit the rule.

The same sort of thing also applies to THEY.

The French for THEY is the same as for HE and SHE but with an S – ILS or ELLES, depending on whether THEY refers to masculine or feminine things. The form of the verb which goes with THEY is usually pronounced exactly the same as for HE or SHE, though it is spelled differently.

So,

> HE DANCES is IL DANSE

THEY DANCE is ILS DANSENT in the masculine and ELLES DANSENT in the feminine. So, if THEY refers to 'the dogs', say, then you use ILS. If THEY refers to 'the cows', you use ELLES.

If masculine and feminine are mixed, then the masculine form is used. So if THEY refers to 'the dogs and the cows', you use the masculine ILS.

There is one small point to make about this. Because ILS and ELLES when they mean THEY have an S on the end, when they come before a verb beginning with a vowel, the S is pronounced, but as if it were a Z. For instance:

> THEY DANCE is ILS or ELLES DANSENT

But:

> THEY BRING is ILS or ELLES APPORTENT (Z'APORT)

213

NOW COVER UP THE ANSWERS BELOW AND TRANS-
LATE THE FOLLOWING:

(You can write your answers in)

1. WE CARRY THE VINEGAR
2. THEY BRING A LADDER
3. THEY FIND THE SCREWS
4. WE HIRE THE ROPE
5. THEY SHOW THE JEWEL TO THE GIRL

The answers are:

1. NOUS PORTONS LE VINAIGRE
2. ILS (OR ELLES) APPORTENT UNE ÉCHELLE
3. ILS (OR ELLES) TROUVENT LES VIS
4. NOUS LOUONS LA CORDE
5. ILS (OR ELLES) MONTRENT LE BIJOU À LA JEUNE
   FILLE

# ELEMENTARY GRAMMAR

You have learned that the French for WE is NOUS.
The French for WE ARE is NOUS SOMMES

Imagine WE ARE the people who KNEW SOME things.

The French for THEY ARE is ILS or ELLES SONT

Imagine THEY ARE singing a SONG.

Now cover up the answers below and translate the following:

(You can write your answers in)

1. WHERE ARE WE?
2. WHERE ARE THEY?

The answers are:

1. OÙ SOMMES-NOUS?
2. OÙ SONT ILS?

## MORE USEFUL WORDS

### THINK OF EACH IMAGE IN YOUR MIND'S EYE FOR ABOUT TEN SECONDS

○ The French for PARCEL is COLIS
   Imagine a CAULIflower in a parcel.

○ The French for PEBBLE is GALET
   Imagine throwing pebbles into a ship's GALLEY.

○ The French for PENCIL is CRAYON
   Imagine using a CRAYON instead of a pencil to take notes.

○ The French for PIPE (that you smoke) is PIPE
   Imagine you PEEP at a pipe.

○ The French for POCKET is POCHE
   Imagine your mother tells you that you don't look POSH with your hands in your pockets.

○ The French for RADIO is RADIO
   Imagine listening to the radio on top of the Eiffel Tower.

○ The French for TELEVISION is TÉLÉVISION
   Imagine watching a television programme about the Eiffel Tower.

○ The French for RECIPE is RECETTE
   Imagine you have to RE-SET your cooker to cook a new recipe.

○ The French for NYLON is NYLON
   Imagine you KNEEL ON nylon.

○ The French for RING is BAGUE
   Imagine an old BAG containing a diamond ring.

# YOU CAN WRITE YOUR ANSWERS IN

○ What is the English for BAGUE? _____

○ What is the English for NYLON? _____

○ What is the English for RECETTE? _____

○ What is the English for TÉLÉVISION? _____

○ What is the English for RADIO? _____

○ What is the English for POCHE? _____

○ What is the English for PIPE? _____

○ What is the English for CRAYON? _____

○ What is the English for GALET? _____

○ What is the English for COLIS? _____

## TURN BACK FOR THE ANSWERS

## GENDERS

**THINK OF EACH IMAGE IN YOUR MIND'S EYE FOR ABOUT TEN SECONDS**

○ The gender of PARCEL is MASCULINE      LE COLIS
Imagine a boxer opening a parcel.

○ The gender of PEBBLE is MASCULINE      LE GALET
Imagine throwing pebbles at a boxer during a fight.

○ The gender of PENCIL is MASCULINE      LE CRAYON
Imagine a boxer with a pencil stuck behind his ear.

○ The gender of PIPE is FEMININE      LA PIPE
Imagine soaking your pipe in perfume to make it smell sweeter.

○ The gender of POCKET is FEMININE      LA POCHE
Imagine putting a bottle of perfume in your pocket.

○ The gender of RADIO is FEMININE      LA RADIO
Imagine a bottle of perfume on top of your radio.

○ The gender of TELEVISION      LA TÉLÉVISION
is FEMININE
Imagine ads for perfume on television.

○ The gender of RECIPE is FEMININE      LA RECETTE
Imagine a recipe which makes you add perfume to the food.

○ The gender of NYLON is MASCULINE      LE NYLON
Imagine a boxer with nylon underpants.

○ The gender of RING is FEMININE      LA BAGUE
Imagine a diamond ring in a bottle of perfume.

## YOU CAN WRITE YOUR ANSWERS IN

○ What is the gender and French for ring? _____

○ What is the gender and French for nylon? _____

○ What is the gender and French for recipe? _____

○ What is the gender and French for television? _____

○ What is the gender and French for radio? _____

○ What is the gender and French for pocket? _____

○ What is the gender and French for pipe? _____

○ What is the gender and French for pencil? _____

○ What is the gender and French for pebble? _____

○ What is the gender and French for parcel?

## TURN BACK FOR THE ANSWERS

Now cover up the answers below and translate the following:

(You can write your answers in)

1. I DANCED ON THE STRANGE PEBBLES, AND ON THE TELEVISION AND ON THE RADIO

2. MY FIRST PIPE AND MY PENCILS ARE IN MY POCKET

3. I FILL THE SMALL PARCEL, AND I PUT THE RINGS AND A RECIPE IN THE PARCEL

4. I HAVE EATEN THE RENT AND I AM GOING TO KISS THE GUIDE

5. THE DOG IS CARRYING A BIG PARCEL, AND I AM GOING TO READ TO THE BRIDE

The answers are:

1. J'AI DANSÉ SUR LES GALETS BIZARRES, ET SUR LA TÉLÉVISION ET SUR LA RADIO

2. MA PREMIÈRE PIPE ET MES CRAYONS SONT DANS MA POCHE

3. JE REMPLIS LE PETIT COLIS, ET JE METS LES BAGUES ET UNE RECETTE DANS LE COLIS

4. J'AI MANGÉ LE LOYER ET JE VAIS EMBRASSER LE GUIDE

5. LE CHIEN PORTE UN GRAND COLIS, ET JE VAIS LIRE À L'ÉPOUSE

**Note**
This means 'on the television/radio set'. 'On the radio' or 'on the television' in the sense of a programme is A LA RADIO or A LA TELEVISION.

## CAMPING

**THINK OF EACH IMAGE IN YOUR MIND'S EYE FOR ABOUT TEN SECONDS**

○ The French for SHEET is DRAP
Imagine you DRAW the sheet over your head when you are cold.

○ The French for BLANKET is COUVERTURE
Imagine you COVET YOUR sister's blanket.

○ The French for SOAP is SAVON
Imagine asking a dirty child not to SAVE ON the soap.

○ The French for SOAP is SAVON
Imagine asking a dirty child to SAVE ON the soap.

○ The French for SOUVENIR is SOUVENIR
Imagine buying a souvenir of the Eiffel Tower.

○ The French for STAR is ÉTOILE
Imagine you EAT WELL under the stars.

○ The French for STICK is BÂTON.
Imagine an orchestral conductor using an old stick as a BATON.

○ The French for STONE is PIERRE
Imagine throwing stones at a PIER.

○ The French for TAP is ROBINET.
Imagine ROBBING A tap from a sink.

○ The French for TENT is TENTE
Imagine a little child crying, 'I TAN'T get to the tent.'

○ The French for TORCH is LAMPE
Imagine lighting a LAMP and using it as a torch.

# YOU CAN WRITE YOUR ANSWERS IN

○ What is the English for LAMPE? _____

○ What is the English for TENTE? _____

○ What is the English for ROBINET? _____

○ What is the English for PIERRE? _____

○ What is the English for BÂTON? _____

○ What is the English for ÉTOILE? _____

○ What is the English for SOUVENIR? _____

○ What is the English for SAVON? _____

○ What is the English for COUVERTURE? _____

○ What is the English for DRAP? _____

## TURN BACK FOR THE ANSWERS

## GENDERS

**THINK OF EACH IMAGE IN YOUR MIND'S EYE FOR ABOUT TEN SECONDS**

○ The gender of SHEET is MASCULINE     **LE DRAP**
Imagine carrying a dead boxer in a sheet.

○ The gender of COUVERTURE is **LA COUVERTURE**
FEMININE
Imagine spraying perfume on a blanket.

○ The gender of SOAP is MASCULINE     **LE SAVON**
Imagine a boxer smearing himself with
soap.

○ The gender of SOUVENIR is **LE SOUVENIR**
MASCULINE
Imagine a boxer being given a souvenir of
his fight.

○ The gender of STAR is FEMININE     **L'ÉTOILE (f)**
Imagine putting perfume on yourself under
the stars.

○ The gender of STICK is MASCULINE     **LE BÂTON**
Imagine a boxer beating his opponent with
a stick.

○ The gender of STONE is FEMININE     **LA PIERRE**
Imagine spraying stones with perfume.

○ The gender of TAP is MASCULINE     **LE ROBINET**
Imagine you put a boxer under a tap to
bring him round.

○ The gender of TENT is FEMININE     **LA TENTE**
Imagine spraying perfume all over your
tent.

○ The gender of TORCH is FEMININE     **LA LAMPE**
Imagine looking for perfume with a torch.

# YOU CAN WRITE YOUR ANSWERS IN

○ What is the gender and French for torch? _____

○ What is the gender and French for tent? _____

○ What is the gender and French for tap? _____

○ What is the gender and French for stone? _____

○ What is the gender and French for stick? _____

○ What is the gender and French for star? _____

○ What is the gender and French for souvenir? _____

○ What is the gender and French for soap? _____

○ What is the gender and French for blanket? _____

○ What is the gender and French for sheet? _____

## TURN BACK FOR THE ANSWERS

Now cover up the answers below and translate the following:

(You can write your answers in)

1. THIS CLOTH IS THE SHEET, AND THIS PARCEL IS THE SOAP

2. THESE SOUVENIRS ARE VERY VULGAR, BUT THIS TORCH AND THIS BLANKET ARE NOT VULGAR

3. THE GUIDE LIKES ME AND HE LIKES YOU ALSO

4. THESE TENTS ARE DIRTY, AND THE STARS ARE VERY DISTANT

5. THE UNCLE CARRIES THE STICKS AND MY STONES IN THE TENT. HE IS NOT CARRYING THE TAP

The answers are:

1. CETTE ÉTOFFE EST LE DRAP, ET CE COLIS EST LE SAVON

2. CES SOUVENIRS SONT TRÈS VULGAIRES, MAIS CETTE LAMPE ET CETTE COUVERTURE NE SONT PAS VULGAIRES

3. LE GUIDE M'AIME ET IL VOUS AIME AUSSI

4. CES TENTES SONT SALES, ET LES ÉTOILES SONT TRÈS LOINTAINES

5. L'ONCLE PORTE LES BÂTONS ET MES PIERRES DANS LA TENTE. IL NE PORTE PAS LE ROBINET

## SEVEN MORE WORDS

**THINK OF EACH IMAGE IN YOUR MIND'S EYE FOR ABOUT TEN SECONDS**

○ The French for IRON is FER
  Imagine iron is a FERROUS metal.

○ The French for STEEL is ACIER
  Imagine watching someone who turned to steel AS HE Ate steel plates.

○ The French for COOKER is RÉCHAUD
  Imagine there is nothing RACIAL in owning a cooker.

○ The French for SAUCEPAN is CASSEROLE
  Imagine you make CASSEROLES in saucepans.

○ The French for CARDBOARD is CARTON
  Imagine a cardboard CARTON.

○ The French for HISTORY is HISTOIRE
  Imagine history is the study of EASTERN Wars.

○ The French for GEOGRAPHY is GÉOGRAPHIE
  Imagine your geography teacher taking you to the Eiffel Tower.

## YOU CAN WRITE YOUR ANSWERS IN

○ What is the English for GÉOGRAPHIE? _____

○ What is the English for HISTOIRE? _____

○ What is the English for CARTON? _____

○ What is the English for CASSEROLE? _____

○ What is the English for RÉCHAUD? _____

○ What is the English for ACIER? _____

○ What is the English for FER? _____

## TURN BACK FOR THE ANSWERS

## GENDERS

**THINK OF EACH IMAGE IN YOUR MIND'S EYE FOR ABOUT TEN SECONDS**

○ The gender of IRON is MASCULINE             **LE FER**
  Imagine a boxer with iron in his gloves.

○ The gender of STEEL is MASCULINE       **L'ACIER (m)**
  Imagine a boxer with a steel jaw.

○ The gender of COOKER is MASCULINE     **LE RÉCHAUD**
  Imagine a boxer sitting on a cooker.

○ The gender of SAUCEPAN is            **LA CASSEROLE**
  FEMININE
  Imagine putting perfume in a saucepan.

○ The gender of CARDBOARD is           **LE CARTON**
  MASCULINE
  Imagine a cardboard box full of perfume
  bottles.

○ The gender of HISTORY is FEMININE     **L'HISTOIRE (f)**
  Imagine a talk on the history of perfume
  making.

○ The gender of GEOGRAPHY is        **LA GÉOGRAPHIE**
  FEMININE
  Imagine seeing where perfume is made as
  part of a geography lesson.

## YOU CAN WRITE YOUR ANSWERS IN

○ What is the gender and French for
geography?                                      _____

○ What is the gender and French for history?    _____

○ What is the gender and French for
cardboard?                                      _____

○ What is the gender and French for
saucepan?                                       _____

○ What is the gender and French for cooker?     _____

○ What is the gender and French for steel?      _____

○ What is the gender and French for iron?       _____


## TURN BACK FOR THE ANSWERS

## THREE MORE LANGUAGES

## THINK OF EACH IMAGE IN YOUR MIND'S EYE FOR ABOUT TEN SECONDS

○ The French for SPANISH is ESPAGNOL
  Imagine a SPANIEL is Spanish.

○ The French for French is FRANÇAIS
  Imagine FRIENDS SAY French is easy.

○ The French for GERMAN is ALLEMAND
  Imagine sending ALMONDS to Germany.

**YOU CAN WRITE YOUR ANSWERS IN**

○ What is the English for ESPAGNOL?  _____

○ What is the English for FRANÇAIS?  _____

○ What is the English for ALLEMAND?  _____

**TURN BACK FOR THE ANSWERS**

## YOU CAN WRITE YOUR ANSWERS IN

○ What is the French for Spanish?　　　　＿＿＿＿＿＿＿

○ What is the French for French?　　　　＿＿＿＿＿＿＿

○ What is the French for German?　　　　＿＿＿＿＿＿＿

**TURN BACK FOR THE ANSWERS**

Now cover up the answers below and translate the following:

(You can write your answers in)

1. HE LIVES IN A SAUCEPAN AND HE SMOKES ON THE COOKER

2. SHE FINDS HIM, BUT SHE LIKES HISTORY AND GEOGRAPHY

3. THE IRON IS FRENCH, THE STEEL IS SPANISH, AND THE CARDBOARD IS GERMAN

4. SHE BRINGS THE BOTTLE AND SHE CATCHES THE BLACK ICE

5. THE GERMAN FISH IS ELEGANT

The answers are:

1. IL HABITE DANS UNE CASSEROLE ET IL FUME SUR LE RÉCHAUD

2. ELLE LE TROUVE, MAIS ELLE AIME L'HISTOIRE ET LA GÉOGRAPHIE

3. LE FER EST FRANÇAIS, L'ACIER EST ESPAGNOL, ET LE CARTON EST ALLEMAND

4. ELLE APPORTE LA BOUTEILLE ET ELLE ATTRAPPE LE VERGLAS

5. LE POISSON ALLEMAND EST ÉLÉGANT

## Section 11    USEFUL PHRASES

**THINK OF EACH IMAGE IN YOUR MIND'S EYE FOR ABOUT TEN SECONDS**

○ The French for HELLO is BONJOUR
Imagine BON is GOOD, JOUR is DAY – HELLO is GOOD DAY.

○ The French for GOOD EVENING is BONSOIR
Imagine you SWEAR in the evening.

○ The French for HOW ARE YOU? is COMMENT ALLEZ-VOUS?
Imagine asking, 'ARE YOU having an ALLEY-VIEW?'
(A VIEW DOWN AN ALLEY)
Note: COMMENT is HOW; so COMMENT ALLEZ-VOUS? is HOW ARE YOU.

○ The French for VERY WELL is TRÈS BIEN
Imagine VERY is TRÈS, WELL is BIEN, so VERY WELL is TRÈS BIEN.

○ The French for SEE YOU SOON is À BIENTÔT
Imagine saying, 'I'VE BEEN TO town – see you soon.'

## YOU CAN WRITE YOUR ANSWERS IN

○ What is the English for À BIENTÔT?         _____

○ What is the English for TRÈS BIEN?       _____

○ What is the English for COMMENT
ALLEZ-VOUS?        _____

○ What is the English for BONSOIR?       _____

○ What is the English for BONJOUR?       _____

TURN BACK FOR THE ANSWERS

238

# COVER UP THE LEFT HAND PAGE

○ **What is the French for see you soon?** _____

○ **What is the French for very well?** _____

○ **What is the French for how are you?** _____

○ **What is the French for good evening?** _____

○ **What is the French for hello?** _____

**TURN BACK FOR THE ANSWERS**

Now cover up the answers below and translate the folllowing:

(You can write your answers in)

1.  HELLO, THE TOWN IS DISTANT
2.  GOOD EVENING, WHERE IS THE BRIDE?
3.  HOW ARE YOU? VERY WELL
4.  MY UNCLE IS POOR. SEE YOU SOON
5.  I SAY TO THE ARCHITECT, 'HOW ARE YOU?'

The answers are:

1.  BONJOUR, LA VILLE EST LOINTAINE
2.  BONSOIR, OÙ EST L'ÉPOUSE?
3.  COMMENT ALLEZ-VOUS? TRÈS BIEN
4.  MON ONCLE EST PAUVRE. À BIENTÔT
5.  JE DIS À L'ARCHITECTE, 'COMMENT ALLEZ-VOUS?'

## MORE USEFUL PHRASES

## THINK OF EACH IMAGE IN YOUR MIND'S EYE FOR ABOUT TEN SECONDS

○ The French for HAVE A GOOD JOURNEY is BON VOYAGE
  Imagine a VOYAGE is a journey.

○ The French for GOOD LUCK is BONNE CHANCE
  Imagine luck is a CHANCY business.

○ The French for SEE YOU TOMORROW is À DEMAIN
  Imagine I'm seeing A DEMON tomorrow.

○ The French for GOODBYE is AU REVOIR
  Imagine saying, 'Goodbye, I'm jumping in A RIVER.'

○ The French for HERE IS is VOICI
  Imagine here is someone FUSSY.

## YOU CAN WRITE THE ANSWERS IN

○ What is the English for VOICI? _____

○ What is the English for AU REVOIR? _____

○ What is the English for À DEMAIN? _____

○ What is the English for BONNE
CHANCE? _____

○ What is the English for BON VOYAGE? _____

### TURN BACK FOR THE ANSWERS

COVER UP THE LEFT HAND PAGE

○ What is the French for here is? _____

○ What is the French for goodbye? _____

○ What is the French for see you tomorrow? _____

○ What is the French for good luck? _____

○ What is the English for have a good
journey? _____

## TURN BACK FOR THE ANSWERS

**Note**
VOICI can also mean 'here are'.

Now cover up the answers below and translate the following:

(You can write your answers in)

1. I WRITE TO MY RELATION, 'HAVE A GOOD JOURNEY'
2. I SAY TO THE HAMMER, 'GOOD LUCK'
3. HELLO MICHELLE, SEE YOU TOMORROW
4. GOODBYE FRED, AND GOOD LUCK
5. HERE IS THE JEWEL AND HERE IS THE BOX

The answers are:

1. J'ÉCRIS À MON PARENT, 'BON VOYAGE'
2. JE DIS AU MARTEAU, 'BONNE CHANCE'
3. BONJOUR MICHELLE, À DEMAIN
4. AU REVOIR FRED, ET BONNE CHANCE
5. VOICI LE BIJOU ET VOICI LA BOÎTE

## SOME MORE USEFUL PHRASES

### THINK OF EACH IMAGE IN YOUR MIND'S EYE FOR ABOUT TEN SECONDS

○ The French for IS THERE? is Y A-T-IL?
Imagine asking, 'Is there a YACHT? I'LL buy it.'

○ The French for HOW FAR IS IT? is C'EST À QUELLE DISTANCE?
Imagine DISTANCE is FAR, C'EST À QUELLE is AT WHAT so C'EST À QUELLE DISTANCE is AT WHAT FAR.

○ The French for MAY I HAVE? is POURRAIS-JE AVOIR?
Imagine asking, 'The POUREES YOU HAVE ARE delicious, may I have some?'

○ The French for THAT'S FINE is C'EST PARFAIT
Imagine PARFAIT is PERFECT, so C'EST PARFAIT is THAT'S FINE.

○ The French for THANKS FOR YOUR TROUBLE is MERCI DU DÉRANGEMENT
Imagine someone troubled and DERANGED.

## YOU CAN WRITE YOUR ANSWERS IN

○ What is the English for MERCI DU DÉRANGEMENT? _____

○ What is the English for C'EST PARFAIT? _____

○ What is the English for POURRAIS-JE AVOIR? _____

○ What is the English for C'EST À QUELLE DISTANCE? _____

○ What is the English for Y A-T-IL? _____

TURN BACK FOR THE ANSWERS

246

## COVER UP THE LEFT HAND PAGE

○ What is the French for thanks for your trouble? _____

○ What is the French for that's fine? _____

○ What is the French for may I have? _____

○ What is the French for how far is it? _____

○ What is the French for is there? _____

TURN BACK FOR THE ANSWERS

**Note**
YA-T-IL? Can also mean 'are there'.

Now cover up the answers below and translate the following:

(You can write your answers in)

1. IS THERE A HOLE IN YOUR CLOTH?
2. I RUN TO PARIS. HOW FAR IS IT?
3. MAY I HAVE A SPARK PLUG?
4. THE GARDENER WAS VULGAR. THAT'S FINE
5. MY AUNT IS HEALTHY. THANKS FOR YOUR TROUBLE

The answers are:

1. Y A-T-IL UN TROU DANS VOTRE ÉTOFFE?
2. JE COURS À PARIS. C'EST À QUELLE DISTANCE?
3. POURRAIS-JE AVOIR UNE BOUGIE?
4. LE JARDINIER ÉTAIT VULGAIRE. C'EST PARFAIT
5. MA TANTE EST SAINE. MERCI DU DÉRANGEMENT

## SOME MORE USEFUL PHRASES

**THINK OF EACH IMAGE IN YOUR MIND'S EYE FOR ABOUT TEN SECONDS**

○ The French for DO YOU SPEAK ENGLISH? is PARLEZ-VOUS ANGLAIS?
Imagine PARLEZ is SPEAK, VOUS is YOU, ANGLAIS is ENGLISH.

○ The French for SPEAK SLOWLY is PARLEZ LENTEMENT
Imagine SPEAK is PARLEZ, SLOWLY is LENTEMENT.

○ The French for I DON'T UNDERSTAND is JE NE COMPRENDS PAS
Imagine COMPRENDS is UNDERSTAND.

○ The French for WHAT'S THE MATTER? is QU'EST-CE QU'IL Y A?
Imagine you are so ILL YOU ask, 'What's the matter?'

○ The French for CAN YOU HELP ME? is POUVEZ-VOUS M'AIDER?
Imagine saying, 'I am in a POOR WAY MY DEAR – can you help me?'

## YOU CAN WRITE YOUR ANSWERS IN

○ What is the English for POUVEZ-VOUS
   M'AIDER? _____

○ What is the English for QU'EST-CE QU'IL
   Y A? _____

○ What is the English for JE NE
   COMPRENDS PAS? _____

○ What is the English for PARLEZ
   LENTEMENT? _____

○ What is the English for PARLEZ-VOUS
   ANGLAIS? _____

TURN BACK FOR THE ANSWERS

250

# COVER UP THE LEFT HAND PAGE

○ What is the French for can you help me? _____

○ What is the French for what's the matter? _____

○ What is the French for I don't understand? _____

○ What is the French for speak slowly? _____

○ What is the French for do you speak
English? _____

TURN BACK FOR THE ANSWERS

Now cover up the answers below and translate the following:

(You can write your answers in)

1. DO YOU SPEAK ENGLISH? VERY WELL
2. SPEAK SLOWLY PLEASE. I HAVE A PENCIL
3. WHAT'S THE MATTER? I AM WEAK
4. I AM AN UNCLE. I DON'T UNDERSTAND THE BIBLE
5. CAN YOU HELP ME? THE NURSE IS PERFECT

The answers are:

1. PARLEZ-VOUS ANGLAIS? TRÈS BIEN
2. PARLEZ LENTEMENT S'IL VOUS PLAÎT. J'AI UN CRAYON
3. QU'EST-CE QU'IL Y A? JE SUIS FAIBLE
4. JE SUIS UN ONCLE. JE NE COMPRENDS PAS LA BIBLE
5. POUVEZ-VOUS M'AIDER? L'INFIRMIÈRE EST PARFAITE

**SOME MORE PHRASES**

**THINK OF EACH IMAGE IN YOUR MIND'S EYE FOR ABOUT TEN SECONDS**

○ The French for I DON'T KNOW is JE NE SAIS PAS
  Imagine asking 'Can JENNY SAY PA', and being told, 'I don't know'.

○ The French for JUST A MINUTE is UNE MINUTE
  Imagine just a minute is ONE MINUTE.

○ The French for COME IN is ENTREZ
  Imagine being told, 'ENTRY – come in'.

○ The French for THIS WAY is PAR ICI
  Imagine it is this way to PARIS.

○ The French for THAT'S ALL is C'EST TOUT
  Imagine I SAID TO you, 'That's all.'

## YOU CAN WRITE THE ANSWERS IN

○ What is the English for C'EST TOUT?     _____

○ What is the English for PAR ICI?     _____

○ What is the English for ENTREZ?     _____

○ What is the English for UNE MINUTE?     _____

○ What is the English for JE NE SAIS PAS?     _____

TURN BACK FOR THE ANSWERS

## COVER UP THE LEFT HAND PAGE

○ What is the French for that's all? _____

○ What is the French for this way? _____

○ What is the French for come in? _____

○ What is the French for just a minute? _____

○ What is the French for I don't know? _____

**TURN BACK FOR THE ANSWERS**

255

Now cover up the answers below and translate the following:

(You can write your answers in)

1. IS THE CHILD MAD? I DON'T KNOW
2. IS HE HERE? JUST A MINUTE
3. COME IN. I HEAR THE DOORBELL
4. WHERE IS THE COAST? THIS WAY
5. TWO GATES PLEASE. THAT'S ALL

The answers are:

1. EST-CE QUE L'ENFANT EST FOU? JE NE SAIS PAS
2. EST-CE QU'IL EST ICI? UNE MINUTE
3. ENTREZ. J'ENTENDS LA SONNETTE
4. OÙ EST LA CÔTE? PAR ICI
5. DEUX BARRIÈRES, S'IL VOUS PLAÎT. C'EST TOUT

Here are a final group of revision sentences. You can now see the range of sensible and useful sentences you can translate. Cover up the answers below and translate the following:

(You can write your answers in)

1. I AM GOING TO THE STATION. IT IS ALMOST TEN O'CLOCK

2. YOUR PANCAKES ARE DELICIOUS

3. WHERE IS THE NURSE?

4. HE SPEAKS FRENCH BUT VERY SLOWLY

5. SHE LIVES AT THE HOTEL

The answers are:

1. JE VAIS À LA GARE. IL EST PRESQUE DIX HEURES

2. VOS CRÊPES SONT DÉLICIEUSES

3. OÙ EST L'INFIRMIÈRE?

4. IL PARLE FRANÇAIS MAIS TRÈS LENTEMENT

5. ELLE HABITE À L'HÔTEL

Now cover up the answers below and translate the following:

(You can write your answers in)

1. I WAS IN THE FIRST TRAIN
2. CAN YOU HELP ME? I HAVE THE MONEY
3. HE IS WRITING A LETTER TO THE WOMAN
4. I HATE HER
5. HER NAPPY IS DIRTY

The answers are:

1. J'ÉTAIS DANS LE PREMIER TRAIN
2. POUVEZ-VOUS M'AIDER? J'AI L'ARGENT
3. IL ÉCRIT UNE LETTRE À LA FEMME
4. JE LA HAIS
5. SA COUCHE EST SALE

Now cover up the answers below and translate the following:

(You can write your answers in)

1. THIS HOUSE HAS A BETTER ROOF
2. SHE WANTS THESE MUSHROOMS ALSO
3. HELLO. WHAT'S THE MATTER? ARE YOU ILL
4. MAY I HAVE THE EXPENSIVE DRESSES?
5. SHE FOUND THE PARCEL BEHIND THE SEAT

The answers are:

1. CETTE MAISON A UN MEILLEUR TOIT
2. ELLE VEUT CES CHAMPIGNONS AUSSI
3. BONJOUR. QU'EST-CE QU'IL Y A? ÊTES-VOUS MALADE?
4. POURRAIS-JE AVOIR LES ROBES CHÈRES?
5. ELLE A TROUVÉE LE COLIS DERRIÈRE LE SIÈGE

Now cover up the answers below and translate the following:

(You can write your answers in)

1. I AM GOING TO SHOW MY PASSPORT AT THE CUSTOMS
2. WE ARE HIRING A NEW CAR
3. THE GRASS IS GREENER HERE
4. I SEE HER IN THE ORCHARD
5. JUST A MINUTE! IS THE BANK OPEN OR IS IT CLOSED?

The answers are:

1. JE VAIS MONTRER MON PASSEPORT À LA DOUANE
2. NOUS LOUONS UNE NOUVELLE VOITURE
3. L'HERBE EST PLUS VERTE ICI
4. JE LA VOIS DANS LE VERGER
5. UNE MINUTE! EST-CE QUE LA BANQUE EST OUVERTE OU EST-CE QU'ELLE EST FERMÉE?

# Section 12   GRAMMAR REVISION

The following section gives the grammar (and vocabulary) which
you should know before you start on Section 1 of this book. If you
find the grammar (or vocabulary) difficult, you should first go
through Linkword I before you start on Further Linkword. If you
have already covered Linkword I you can use this section as a useful revision exercise before you start on Further Linkword.

To revise the contents of this book, you should first revise the
following section then go back to Section I and carry on through to
the end of Section 11. In order to keep the material fresh you should
revise it every few months. However the material learned using
Linkword comes back surprisingly easily after a gap – and for
many people it is quite sufficient to go through the course again a
week or so before going to France.

**Note** The vocabulary which it is assumed you already know is
given in the glossary at the end of this section. The glossary at the
end of the book combines the vocabulary of Linkword I and the
present book.

## THE FIRST REVISION POINT

## ELEMENTARY GRAMMAR

In French, adjectives (like BIG, DIRTY, etc.) change their endings to agree with the gender of the word they go with.

When the word is FEMININE, then you normally add an 'e' to the end of the adjective.

For example,

> PETIT CHIEN (masculine) is LITTLE DOG
> PETITE CHÈVRE (feminine) is LITTLE GOAT
> GRAND TAPIS (masculine) is BIG CARPET
> GRANDE TABLE (feminine) is BIG TABLE

In the MASCULINE, the last consonant is not normally pronounced.

So,

> PETIT is pronounced PeTEE.

However, in the FEMININE, you do pronounce the last consonant.

So,

> PETITE is pronounced PeTEET

Again, GRAND is pronounced GROn

GRANDE is pronounced GROnD

If, however, the adjective already ends in 'e' (for example RAPIDE, SALE, etc.), you make no change in either spelling or pronunciation in the feminine.

Now cover up the answers below and translate the following:

(You can write your answers in)

1. THE CHAIR IS PINK
2. THE WARDROBE IS BLUE
3. THE CUPBOARD IS GREEN
4. THE BED IS HEAVY
5. THE GOOSE IS TIRED

The answers are:

1. LA CHAISE EST ROSE
2. L'ARMOIRE EST BLEUE
3. LE PLACARD EST VERT
4. LE LIT EST LOURD
5. L'OIE EST FATIGUÉE

# ELEMENTARY GRAMMAR

Adjectives in French often come after the noun.

For example,

> BLACK DOG  is  CHIEN NOIR
>
> QUICK CAT  is  CHAT RAPIDE

With one or two exceptions, it is not usually wrong to put the adjectives after the noun.

For example,

> RED TABLE  is  TABLE ROUGE
>
> QUIET COW  is  VACHE TRANQUILLE

Two exceptions are:

> BIG  –  GRAND
>
> SMALL  –  PETIT

which almost always come BEFORE the noun.

For example,

> BIG RABBIT  is  GRAND LAPIN
>
> SMALL CHAIR  is  PETITE CHAISE

Now cover up the answers below and translate the following:

(You can write your answers in)

1. THE BLACK HORSE EATS THE GREEN CHAIR
2. THE LITTLE MOUSE SEES THE BIG DEER

The answers are:

1. LE CHEVAL NOIR MANGE LA CHAISE VERTE
2. LA PETITE SOURIS VOIT LE GRAND CERF

266

## ELEMENTARY GRAMMAR

The French word for I is JE

The French word for AM is SUIS
   Imagine I AM a SWEDE

      To say I AM THE RABBIT you say JE SUIS LE LAPIN

      To say I AM THE DOOR you say JE SUIS LA PORTE


The French word for HE is IL

   Imagine HE is in an EEL.

So,

HE IS  is  IL EST

HE EATS  is  IL MANGE

HE IS TIRED  is  IL EST FATIGUÉ

The French word for SHE is ELLE
   Imagine SHE is HELL to live with.

So,

SHE SEES  is  ELLE VOIT

SHE IS DIRTY  is  ELLE EST SALE

Now cover up the answers below and translate the following:

(You can write your answers in)

1. SHE HAS A NEWSPAPER
2. HE IS EATING AN APPLE

The answers are:

1. ELLE A UN JOURNAL
2. IL MANGE UNE POMME

# ELEMENTARY GRAMMAR

In French you normally make a word plural by adding an 's' at the end, but usually this is not pronounced.

For example the word for skirt (JUPE) is pronounced in the same way, whether singular or plural.

The word for THE in the plural is LES – for both masculine and feminine words.

So,

> THE SKIRTS  is  LES JUPES
>
> THE DOGS  is  LES CHIENS
>
> THE BLACK DOGS  is  LES CHIENS NOIRS

Note that you normally also add an 's' to the end of the adjective, but this is not pronounced either.

PLEASE NOTE that if you have a masculine and a feminine noun together like

> THE DOG AND THE COW ARE SMALL

then 'small' is used in a masculine way – PETITS.

In other words the masculine dominates the feminine.

The French for ARE in sentences like THE DOG AND THE CAT ARE BLACK is SONT

So,

> THE DOG AND THE CAT ARE BLACK
> is  LE CHIEN ET LE CHAT SONT NOIRS

Now cover up the answers below and translate the following:

(You can write your answers in)

1. THE DOCTORS ARE VERY QUICK HERE
2. THE WORKERS AND THE MANAGERS ARE IN THE ROOM

The answers are:

1. LES MÉDECINS SONT TRÈS RAPIDES ICI
2. LES OUVRIERS ET LES DIRECTEURS SONT DANS LA PIÈCE

## ELEMENTARY GRAMMAR

When you want to say THE DOGS EAT or THE CATS EAT and so on, the word for EAT is MANGENT, pronounced like MANGE.

This is also true of the word SEE.

So,

> THE DOGS SEE is LES CHIENS VOIENT

> The word HAVE in THE DOGS HAVE is ONT
> The word WANT in THE DOGS WANT is VEULENT

So,

| | | |
|---|---|---|
| THE DOG WANTS | is | LE CHIEN VEUT |
| THE DOGS AND THE CATS WANT | is | LES CHIENS ET LES CHATS VEULENT |

| | | |
|---|---|---|
| THE DOGS WANT | is | LES CHIENS VEULENT |
| THE DOGS SEE | is | LES CHIENS VOIENT |
| THE DOGS EAT | is | LES CHIENS MANGENT |
| THE DOGS HAVE | is | LES CHIENS ONT |

Now cover up the answers below and translate the following:

(You can write your answers in)

1. THE BOYS ARE EATING THE FOOD
2. THE WIVES WANT A HOTEL

The answers are:

1. LES GARÇONS MANGENT LA NOURRITURE
2. LES FEMMES VEULENT UN HÔTEL

## ELEMENTARY GRAMMAR

When you ask questions in French, you can always do so by keeping the same word order as normal, but putting the words EST-CE QUE first.

Imagine you ASK A question.

So,

|  |  |
|---|---|
| THE DOGS ARE BLACK is | LES CHIENS SONT NOIRS |
| ARE THE DOGS BLACK? is | EST-CE QUE LES CHIENS SONT NOIRS? |
| THE RESTAURANT IS DIRTY is | LE RESTAURANT EST SALE |
| IS THE RESTAURANT DIRTY? is | EST-CE QUE LE RESTAURANT EST SALE? |

However, if the word which follows EST-CE QUE begins with a vowel then the 'E' of QUE is dropped.

For example,

HE IS UGLY is IL EST LAID

IS HE UGLY? is EST-CE QU'IL EST LAID?

Now cover up ther answers below and translate the following:

(You can write your answers in)

1. IS THE SKIRT UNDER THE BED?
2. ARE THE SHOES IN THE CUPBOARD?

The answers are:

1. EST-CE QUE LA JUPE EST SOUS LE LIT?
2. EST-CE QUE LES CHAUSSURES SONT DANS LE
   PLACARD?

# ELEMENTARY GRAMMAR: TELLING THE TIME (1)

The French for HOUR is HEURE, which is feminine.

The French for WHAT? in the feminine is QUELLE (pronounced KEL)

Imagine thinking, 'WHAT? KILL HER!'

To say WHAT TIME IS IT? you simply say WHAT HOUR IS IT? In French this is:

> QUELLE HEURE EST-IL?

To answer the question in French, for example IT IS ONE O'CLOCK, IT IS TWO O'CLOCK, the literal translation is IT IS ONE HOUR, IT IS TWO HOURS, and so on.

So,

    IT IS ONE O'CLOCK  is  IT IS ONE HOUR
                           (IL EST UNE HEURE)

    IT IS TWO O'CLOCK  is  IT IS TWO HOURS
                           (IL EST DEUX HEURES)

To say IT IS TWELVE O'CLOCK (midday) you say IL EST MIDI
       IT IS TWELVE O'CLOCK (midnight) is IL EST MINUIT

and so on.

## TELLING THE TIME (2)

When you want to say IT IS FIVE *PAST* SEVEN or TEN *PAST* EIGHT or TWENTY *PAST* NINE or TWENTY-FIVE *PAST* TEN, then you simply put the number of minutes after the hour.

For example,

SEVEN HOURS FIVE (SEPT HEURES  is  FIVE PAST
CINQ)   SEVEN

TEN HOURS TEN (DIX HEURES DIX)  is  TEN PAST
TEN

So, to say IT IS FIVE PAST ELEVEN, you just say IL EST ONZE HEURES CINQ.

To say IT IS QUARTER PAST or HALF PAST THE HOUR you simply say, for example, SEVEN HOURS AND QUARTER or SEVEN HOURS AND HALF.

So,

HALF PAST FIVE  is  CINQ HEURES ET DEMIE

QUARTER PAST THREE  is  TROIS HEURES ET
QUART

## TELLING THE TIME (3)

If you want to say IT IS FIVE TO SIX, and so on then in French you say:

> IT IS SIX HOURS MINUS FIVE.

The French for MINUS (or LESS) is MOINS

  Imagine you MOAN for LESS.

So,

>  IT IS FIVE TO SEVEN  is  IT IS SEVEN HOURS MINUS FIVE which in French is IL EST SEPT HEURES MOINS CINQ

>  IT IS TWENTY TO NINE  is  IT IS NINE HOURS MINUS TWENTY which in French is IL EST NEUF HEURES MOINS VINGT

There is one final point:

When you want to say IT IS QUARTER TO TEN or QUARTER TO ELEVEN, and so on, the 'quarter' is LE QUART.

So,

>  IT IS QUARTER TO FOUR  is  IL EST QUATRE HEURES
>                                    MOINS LE QUART

Now cover up the answers below and translate the following:

(You can write your answers in)

1. IT IS QUARTER TO FOUR
2. IT IS TEN PASI SIX

The answers are:

1. IL EST QUATRE HEURES MOINS LE QUART
2. IL EST SIX HEURES DIX

## ELEMENTARY GRAMMAR

The French word for YES is OUI

   Imagine thinking, 'YES WE want it.'

The French word for NO is NON

   Imagine thinking 'NO! NO!'

When you want to say NOT in French, for example, SHE DOES NOT EAT, you say SHE EATS NOT.

The word for NOT is PAS

   Imagine thinking, 'NOT my PA again drunk.'

However, you must also add the word NE.

So,

> SHE EATS NOT or SHE DOES NOT EAT is ELLE NE MANGE PAS
>
> HE DOES NOT WANT THE CABBAGE is HE WANTS NOT THE CABBAGE, which is IL NE VEUT PAS LE CHOU
>
> THE DOG DOES NOT EAT THE CAT is THE DOG EATS NOT THE CAT, which is LE CHIEN NE MANGE PAS LE CHAT

There is one final point:

If the NE comes before a word which starts with a vowel (for example, EST) then NE becomes N' – N-apostrophE

So,

> IL NE MANGE PAS is HE DOES NOT EAT

but

> HE IS NOT BIG is IL N'EST PAS GRAND

Now cover up the answers below and translate the following:

(You can write your answers in)

1. NO, THE FISH IS NOT HOT
2. THE HUSBAND IS NOT THE BOSS

The answers are:

1. NON, LE POISSON N'EST PAS CHAUD
2. LE MARI N'EST PAS LE PATRON

# ELEMENTARY GRAMMAR: WAS AND WERE

The French for the words WAS and WERE are pronounced AYTAY, although they are spelt differently.

ÉTAIT is WAS.

ÉTAIENT is WERE.

Imagine wishing I WAS EIGHTY again.

So,

THE DOG WAS BLUE  is  LE CHIEN ÉTAIT BLEU

THE DOGS WERE BLUE  is  LES CHIENS ÉTAIENT BLEUS

I WAS is J'ÉTAIS

Now cover up the answers below and translate the following:

(You can write your answers in)

1. THE TOILETS WERE CLEAN
2. THE GIRL WAS TIRED

The answers are:

1. LES TOILETTES ÉTAIENT PROPRES
2. LA JEUNE FILLE ÉTAIT FATIGUÉE

## ELEMENTARY GRAMMAR

The words WHERE, WHY, WHEN, HOW are sometimes used with the word EST-CE QUE when asking questions.

As you learned earlier, you use EST-CE QUE when you want to turn a sentence that already exists into a question.

For example,

IS THE WORKER BLUE? is a question, so you should put EST-CE QUE in front:

EST-CE QUE L'OUVRIER EST BLEU?

| WHY IS THE WORKER BLUE? | is | POURQUOI EST-CE QUE L'OUVRIER EST BLEU? |
| WHEN IS THE ROOF DIRTY? | is | QUAND EST-CE QUE LE TOIT EST SALE? |

Here is another example:

HOW DOES THE BOSS WANT THE FISH? is COMMENT EST-CE QUE LE PATRON VEUT LE POISSON?

However, if you just want to say WHERE IS or WHERE ARE, you simply say:

OÙ EST or OÙ SONT without the EST-CE QUE.

So,

WHERE IS THE BOSS? is OÙ EST LE PATRON?

Now cover up the answers below and translate the following:

(You can write your answers in)

1. WHERE ARE THE PLATES?
2. WHY ARE THE KNIVES DIRTY?

The answers are:

1. OÙ SONT LES ASSIETTES?
2. POURQUOI EST-CE QUE LES COUTEAUX SONT SALES?

# ELEMENTARY GRAMMAR

The French for YOU is VOUS

Imagine YOU VIEW something.

In French a verb such as EAT, SEE or WANT nearly always has an ending EZ (pronounced AY) when you use the word YOU.

So,

I EAT is JE MANGE

YOU EAT is VOUS MANGEZ

I SEE is JE VOIS

YOU SEE is VOUS VOYEZ

There are some verbs which change slightly in the middle when used with the word VOUS.

For example,

I WANT is JE VEUX

YOU WANT is VOUS VOULEZ

It adds an EZ, but the EUX becomes OUL.

Do not worry about this, however, you will pick it up as you go along.

Now cover up the answers below and translate the following:

(You can write your answers in)

1. YOU WANT THE PEAR
2. YOU HAVE THE PETROL

The answers are:

1. VOUS VOULEZ LA POIRE
2. VOUS AVEZ L'ESSENCE

## ELEMENTARY GRAMMAR

To use the words ON, UNDER, and so on, is very simple. You usually use them in the same way as in English.

So,

> ON THE TABLE   is   SUR LA TABLE
>
> UNDER THE CHAIR   is   SOUS LA CHAISE

Now cover up the answers below and translate the following:

(You can write your answers in)

1. THE MEAT IS ON THE TABLE
2. THE JACKET IS UNDER THE SKIRT

The answers are:

1. LA VIANDE EST SUR LA TABLE
2. LA VESTE EST SOUS LA JUPE

## ELEMENTARY GRAMMAR

You will remember that if you want to say:

> HE DOES NOT EAT  or  HE DOES NOT WANT
> THE FISH           THE CUSTOMS

you say,

> IL NE MANGE PAS  or  IL NE VEUT PAS
> LE POISSON         LA DOUANE

However, to say

> HE WANTS THE CAR, NOT THE BOAT

you simply say PAS for NOT:

> IL VEUT L'AUTO, PAS LE BATEAU

Now cover up the answers below and translate the following:

(You can write your answers in)

1. SHE HAS THE FORKS NOT THE KNIVES
2. I HAVE THE PASSPORT BUT NOT THE TICKET

The answers are:

1. ELLE A LES FOURCHETTES PAS LES COUTEAUX
2. J'AI LE PASSEPORT MAIS PAS LE BILLET

# ELEMENTARY GRAMMAR

To make a word like 'quickly' from 'quick', or 'quietly' from 'quiet', you normally take the feminine form of the word and add MENT (MOn).

So,

QUICK is RAPIDE

and QUICKLY is RAPIDEMENT

HEAVY is LOURD

and HEAVILY is LOURDEMENT

Now cover up the answers below and translate the following:

(You can write your answers in)

1. THE DOG IS EATING QUICKLY
2. I AM SPEAKING SLOWLY

The answers are:

1. LE CHIEN MANGE RAPIDEMENT
2. JE PARLE LENTEMENT

## ELEMENTARY GRAMMAR

In French, words like MY, HIS, etc. have two forms: one in the masculine and one in the feminine.

For example,

MY DOG is MON CHIEN

MY TABLE is MA TABLE

In other words, the MY is masculine if it goes with a masculine word, but it is feminine if it goes with a feminine word.

So,

MY DOG IS BLACK is MON CHIEN EST NOIR
(masculine)

MY TABLE IS BLACK is MA TABLE EST NOIRE
(feminine)

To remember that MY is MON:
Imagine thinking, 'MY doesn't HE MOAN!'

To remember that MY is MA:
Imagine thinking, 'SHE is MY MA.'

The same rule is also true for HIS.

The French for HIS is SON (SOHn).
Imagine him singing HIS SONG.

The French for HIS when it goes with a feminine word is SA
Imagine his SIghing at a beautiful girl.

So,

HIS DOG IS BLACK is SON CHIEN EST NOIR
(masculine)

HIS TABLE IS BLACK is SA TABLE EST NOIRE
(feminine)

You must remember that HIS is feminine when it is used with a feminine noun. Similarly, the word HER is masculine when it goes with a masculine noun.

Now cover up the answers below and translate the following:

(You can write your answers in)

1. MY DOOR IS RED
2. MY CAT IS DIRTY

The answers are:

1. MA PORTE EST ROUGE
2. MON CHAT EST SALE

## ELEMENTARY GRAMMAR

HER works like HIS. The French for HER is SON when it goes with a masculine noun, and SA when it goes with a feminine noun.

So,

HER DOG IS BLACK    is  SON CHIEN EST NOIR

HER TABLE IS BLACK    is  SA TABLE EST NOIRE

ITS is also the same as HIS and HER.

So,

ITS DOG IS BLACK  is  SON CHIEN EST NOIR

ITS TABLE IS BLACK  is  SA TABLE EST NOIRE

Now cover up the answers below and translate the following:

(You can write your answers in)

1. HIS SISTER IS YOUNG
2. HER FATHER IS VERY QUIET

The answers are:

1. SA SOEUR EST JEUNE
2. SON PÈRE EST TRÈS TRANQUILLE

## ELEMENTARY GRAMMAR

The French for YOUR as in 'YOUR TABLE' is VOTRE

   Imagine you are a VOTER for YOUR candidate.

The French for OUR is NOTRE

   Remember, NOTRE Dame is the church of OUR Lady.

This is the same for masculine and feminine words.

Now cover up the answers below and translate the following:

(You can write your answers in)

1. OUR MOTHER IS HERE
2. YOUR SON IS THIN

The answers are:

1. NOTRE MÈRE EST ICI
2. VOTRE FILS EST MINCE

# ELEMENTARY GRAMMAR

You have just seen that MY, HIS, HER are masculine or feminine, depending on the word they go with.

This is very tricky and you will make mistakes.

Another slight complication is that the words for MY, and so on, change if the word they go with is plural.

So,

### MY DOGS is MES CHIENS

Imagine saying 'MAY I see MY dogs?'

### YOUR DOGS is VOS CHIENS

Imagine your VOtes are here.

### HIS DOGS is SES CHIENS
### HER DOGS is SES CHIENS

Imagine saying, 'Where are HIS/HER dogs?'

### OUR DOGS is NOS CHIENS (NO)

Imagine a Scot saying, 'It's NO our dogs.'

So,

|              |    |                 |
|-------------:|:--:|:----------------|
| MY           | is | MON, MA or MES  |
| HIS or HER   | is | SON, SA or SES  |
| YOUR         | is | VOTRE or VOS    |
| OUR          | is | NOTRE or NOS    |

|                    |    |                  |
|-------------------:|:--:|:-----------------|
| OUR DOGS ARE DIRTY | is | NOS CHIENS SONT SALES |
| YOUR BANKS ARE CLEAN | is | VOS BANQUES SONT PROPRES |

301

Now cover up the answers below and translate the following:

(You can write your answers in)

1. OUR CATS ARE QUICK
2. YOUR BOYS ARE DIRTY

The answers are:

1. NOS CHATS SONT RAPIDES
2. VOS GARÇONS SONT SALES

## ELEMENTARY GRAMMAR

When you want to say things like THE BOY'S BOOK, in French you must say THE BOOK OF THE BOY, and so on.

The word for OF is DE

   Imagine thinking that this is the book OF DE boy.

To say OF THE you say DE LA if the word following is feminine.

So,

> OF THE MEAT  is  DE LA VIANDE
>
> OF THE MOUTH  is  DE LA BOUCHE

If the word is masculine, OF THE is DU

   Imagine asking, 'DO you have to say OF THE?'

So,

> OF THE DOG  is  DU CHIEN
>
> OF THE ARM  is  DU BRAS

Also, of course:

> THE BOY'S MOUTH  is  THE MOUTH OF THE BOY
> (LA BOUCHE DU GARÇON)
>
> THE GIRL'S ARM  is  THE ARM OF THE GIRL
> (LE BRAS DE LA JEUNE FILLE)

Now cover up the answers below and translate the following:

(You can write your answers in)

1. THE BOY'S SISTER IS VERY PRETTY
2. THE WIFE'S CUP IS FULL

The answers are:

1. LA SOEUR DU GARÇON EST TRÈS JOLIE
2. LA TASSE DE LA FEMME EST PLEINE

## ELEMENTARY GRAMMAR

When you want to say OF THE AMBULANCE, you say DE L'AMBULANCE.

In other words, for words which begin with a vowel in French, you always say DE L' when you mean OF THE.

Finally, when the word is plural, such as OF THE DOGS, then the word for OF THE is DES whether it is masculine or feminine.

So,

OF THE DOGS is DES CHIENS

Now cover up the answers below and translate the following:

(You can write your answers in)

1. THE ROOF OF THE AMBULANCE IS BLUE
2. THE LEG OF THE DOGS IS BLUE

The answers are:

1. LE TOIT DE L'AMBULANCE EST BLEU
2. LA JAMBE DES CHIENS EST BLEUE

# GLOSSARY TO LINKWORD I

| | | | |
|---|---|---|---|
| a (an) | un/une | cat | le chat |
| accountant | le comptable | ceiling | le plafond |
| am | suis | chair | la chaise |
| ambulance | l'ambulance (f) | cheese | le fromage |
| and | et | chemist's shop | la pharmacie |
| angry | fâché | cheque | le chèque |
| animal | l'animal (m) | cinema | le cinéma |
| apple | la pomme | clean | propre |
| are (you) | êtes | clock | la pendule |
| are (they) | sont | closed | fermé |
| arm | le bras | clothes | les vêtements |
| armchair | le fauteuil | | (m) |
| at | à | coffee | le café |
| back | le dos | cold | froid |
| baker's shop | la boulangerie | contract | le contrat |
| bank | la banque | countryside | la campagne |
| beach | la plage | cow | la vache |
| bean | le haricot | cup | la tasse |
| because | parce que | cupboard | le placard |
| bed | le lit | curtain | le rideau |
| beer | la bière | customs | la douane |
| big | grand | cutlery | le couvert |
| bill | l'addition (f) | danger | le danger |
| black | noir | daughter | la fille |
| blood | le sang | day | le jour |
| blue | bleu | dear | le cerf |
| boat | le bateau | deep | profond |
| book | le livre | dentist | le dentiste |
| boss | le patron | difficult | difficile |
| boy | le garçon | dinner | le dîner |
| bread | le pain | dirty | sale |
| bridge | le pont | doctor | le médecin |
| brother | le frère | dog | le chien |
| but | mais | door | la porte |
| butcher's shop | la boucherie | dress | la robe |
| butter | le beurre | drink | la boisson |
| cabbage | le chou | dry | sec (sèche) |
| camera | l'appareil (m) | duck | le canard |
| camera film | la pellicule | easy | facile |
| car | l'auto (f) | eat (I) | mange |
| carpet | le tapis | eat (they) | mangent |
| cash till | la caisse | eat (you) | mangez |

307

| | | | |
|---|---|---|---|
| eats | mange | hen | la poule |
| egg | l'oeuf (m) | her | son/sa/ses |
| elephant | l'éléphant (m) | here | ici |
| empty | vide | high | haut |
| engaged | occupé | his | son/sa/ses |
| entrance | l'entrée (f) | holidays | les vacances (f) |
| exit | la sortie | horse | le cheval |
| expensive | cher | hospital | l'hôpital (m) |
| factory | l'usine (f) | hot | chaud |
| father | le père | hotel | l'hôtel (m) |
| fire! | au feu! | hour | l'heure (f) |
| firm | la compagnie | house | la maison |
| fish | le poisson | how | comment |
| floor | le plancher | husband | le mari |
| flower | la fleur | I | je |
| fly | la mouche | ice | la glace |
| food | la nourriture | ice cream | la glace |
| forest | la forêt | illness | la maladie |
| fork | la fourchette | in | dans |
| fruit | le fruit | inn | l'auberge (f) |
| full | plein | insect | l'insecte (m) |
| garage | le garage | is | est |
| garden | le jardin | its | son/sa/ses |
| garlic | l'aïl (m) | jack | le cric |
| girl | la jeune fille | jacket | la veste |
| glass | le verre | key | la clef |
| go (I) | vais | kitchen | la cuisine |
| goat | la chèvre | knife | le couteau |
| gold(en) | doré | left | la gauche |
| good | bon | leg | la jambe |
| goose | l'oie (f) | letter | la lettre |
| grass | l'herbe (f) | lettuce | la salade |
| green | vert | like (I) | aime |
| grey | gris | lobster | le homard |
| half | | lunch | le déjeuner |
|   (of time) | demie | manager | le directeur |
| hand | la main | market | le marché |
| hard | dur | meat | la viande |
| has | a | menu | la carte |
| hat | le chapeau | midday | midi |
| have (I) | ai | midnight | minuit |
| have (they) | ont | milk | le lait |
| have (you) | avez | minute | la minute |
| he | il | mistake | l'erreur (f) |
| heavy | lourd | money | l'argent (m) |
| hedgehog | le hérisson | money | |
| help! | au secours! |   exchange | le change |

308

| | | | |
|---|---|---|---|
| month | le mois | rabbit | le lapin |
| morning | le matin | rain | la pluie |
| mother | la mère | receipt | le reçu |
| mountain | la montagne | red | rouge |
| mouse | la souris | restaurant | le restaurant |
| mouth | la bouche | rib | la côte |
| mushroom | le champignon | right | la droite |
| my | mon/ma/mes | river | la rivière |
| narrow | étroit | road | le route |
| newspaper | le journal | roof | le toit |
| night | la nuit | room | la pièce |
| no | non | salary | le salaire |
| not | pas | salesman | le vendeur |
| of the | du/de la/des | sand | le sable |
| office | le bureau | sea | la mer |
| oil | l'huile (f) | second | la seconde |
| on | sur | secretary | la secrétaire |
| or | ou | see (I) | vois |
| orange (adj) | orange | see (they) | voient |
| our | notre/nos | see (you) | voyez |
| oyster | l'huître (f) | sees | voit |
| pain | la douleur | sell (I) | vends |
| passport | le passeport | she | elle |
| peach | la pêche | sheep | le mouton |
| pear | la poire | shoe | la chaussure |
| pedestrian | le piéton | shop | le magasin |
| pen | le stylo | short | court |
| petrol | l'essence (f) | sister | la soeur |
| piano | le piano | skirt | la jupe |
| picnic | le pique-nique | slow | lent |
| pink | rose | small | petit |
| plate | l'assiette (f) | snail | l'escargot (m) |
| please | s'il vous plaît | snow | la neige |
| police | la police | sock | la chaussette |
| postage stamp | le timbre | son | le fils |
| potato | la pomme de terre | soon | bientôt |
| | | spanner | la clef |
| pretty | joli | speak (I) | parle |
| price | le prix | spoon | la cuiller |
| prize | le prix | staircase | l'escalier (m) |
| pullover | le pullover | station | la gare |
| quarter (of time) | (le) quart | striker | le gréviste |
| | | stupid | stupide |
| quick | rapide | suitcase | la valise |
| quiet | tranquille | sun | le soleil |
| quite | assez | table | la table |

| | | | |
|---|---|---|---|
| tablecloth | la nappe | when | quand |
| telephone | le téléphone | where | où |
| thank you | merci | white | blanc (blanche) |
| the | le/la/les | why | pourquoi |
| theatre | la théâtre | wide | large |
| there | là | wife | la femme or |
| thief | le voleur | | l'épouse |
| thin | mince | window | la fenêtre |
| throat | la gorge | wine | le vin |
| ticket | le billet | with | avec |
| time | le temps | woman | la femme |
| tip | le pourboire | worker | l'ouvrier (m) |
| tired | fatigué | year | l'an (m) |
| to | à | yellow | jaune |
| toilet | la toilette | yes | oui |
| tomato | la tomate | you | vous |
| tongue | la langue | young | jeune |
| towel | la serviette | your | votre/vos |
| town | la ville | | |
| tree | l'arbre (m) | | |
| trousers | le pantalon | **Days of the Week** | |
| trout | la truite | Monday | lundi |
| tyre | le pneu | Tuesday | mardi |
| ugly | laid | Wednesday | mercredi |
| under | sous | Thursday | jeudi |
| underpants | le slip | Friday | vendredi |
| vegetable | le légume | Saturday | samedi |
| very | très | Sunday | dimanche |
| waiter | le garçon | | |
| waitress | la serveuse | | |
| walk | la promenade | | |
| wall | le mur | **Months of the Year** | |
| want (I) | veux | January | janvier |
| want (they) | veulent | February | février |
| want (you) | voulez | March | mars |
| wants | veut | April | avril |
| wardrobe | l'armoire (f) | May | mai |
| was (he, she, | | June | juin |
| it) | était | July | juillet |
| was (I) | étais | August | août |
| wasp | la guêpe | September | septembre |
| water | l'eau (f) | October | octobre |
| week | la semaine | November | novembre |
| were (they) | étaient | December | décembre |
| wet | mouillé | | |
| what time | quelle heure | | |
| is it? | est-il? | | |

310

## Numbers

| | | | |
|---|---|---|---|
| zero | zéro | nine | neuf |
| one | un | ten | dix |
| two | deux | eleven | onze |
| three | trois | twenty | vingt |
| four | quatre | twenty-five | vingt-cinq |
| five | cinq | 12 midnight | minuit |
| six | six | 12 midday | midi |
| seven | sept | | |
| eight | huit | | |

# COMBINED GLOSSARY

| | | | |
|---|---|---|---|
| a (f) | une | attic | la mansarde |
| a (m) | un | August | août |
| accountant | le comptable | aunt | la tante |
| adult | l'adulte (m or f) | autumn | l'automne (m) |
| after | après | back | le dos |
| against | contre | bad (m) | mauvais (m) |
| air | l'air (m) | bad (f) | mauvaise (f) |
| air- | | bag | le sac |
| conditioning | la climatisation | baker | le boulanger |
| alarm clock | le réveil | baker's shop | la boulangerie |
| almost | presque | balcony | le balcon |
| alone | seul | bank | la banque |
| also | aussi | basement | le sous-sol |
| always | toujours | bay | la baie |
| am | suis | beach | la plage |
| am going, I | vais, je | bean | le haricot |
| ambulance | l'ambulance (f) | because | parce que |
| among | parmi | bed | le lit |
| anchor | l'ancre (f) | beer | la bière |
| and | et | before | avant |
| angry | fâché | behind | derrière |
| animal | l'animal (m) | believe, I | crois, je |
| anniversary | l'anniversaire (m) | belt | la ceinture |
| | | bench | le banc |
| answer, I | réponds, je | better | meilleur |
| apple | la pomme | better | meilleure (f) |
| April | avril | between | entre |
| architect | l'architecte (m) | bible | la bible |
| are | sont | big | grand |
| are, they | sont, ils (or elles) | big (f) | grande (f) |
| | | bill | l'addition (f) |
| are, we | sommes, nous | biology | la biologie |
| | | birthday | l'anniversaire (m) |
| are, you | êtes, vous | | |
| arm | le bras | bitter | amer |
| armchair | le fauteuil | black | noir |
| artichoke | l'artichaut (m) | black ice | le verglas |
| ask, I | demande, je | blanket | la couverture |
| asks, he | demande, il | blood | le sang |
| asks, she | demande, elle | blue | bleu |
| asparagus | l'asperge (f) | boarding house | la pension |
| at | à | boat | le bateau |

312

| | | | |
|---|---|---|---|
| bolt | le verrou | cat | le chat |
| book | le livre | catch, I | attrape, j' |
| boring | ennuyeux | cathedral | la cathédrale |
| boring (f) | ennuyeuse (f) | cave | la grotte |
| boss | le patron | ceiling | le plafond |
| bottle | la bouteille | certain | certain |
| box | la boîte | certain (f) | certaine (f) |
| boy | le garçon | chair | la chaise |
| bread | le pain | charming | charmant |
| bride | l'épouse (f) | charming (f) | charmante (f) |
| bridegroom | le marié | cheeky | insolent |
| bridge | le pont | cheeky (f) | insolente (f) |
| bring, I | apporte, j' | cheese | le fromage |
| bring, they (f) | apportent, elles | chemist's shop | la pharmacie |
| | | chemistry | la chimie |
| bring, they (m) | apportent, ils | cheque | le chèque |
| broom | le balai | chicken | le poulet |
| brother | le frère | child | l'enfant (m or f) |
| brush | la brosse | Christmas | Noël (m) |
| building | le bâtiment | cider | le cidre |
| but | mais | cinema | le cinéma |
| butcher | le boucher | citizen | le citoyen |
| butcher's shop | la boucherie | clean | propre |
| butter | le beurre | clear | clair |
| button | le bouton | cliff | la falaise |
| buy, I | achète, j' | climate | le climat |
| cabbage | le chou | clock | la pendule |
| call, I | appelle, j' | closed | fermé |
| camera | l'appareil (m) | cloth | l'étoffe (f) |
| camera film | la pellicule | clothes | les vêtements (m.pl) |
| can you help me? | pouvez-vous m'aider? | coast | la côte |
| car | l'auto (f) | coffee | le café |
| caravan | la caravane | cold | froid |
| cardboard | le carton | cold (f) | froide (f) |
| carpark | le parking | comb | le peigne |
| carpenter | le menuisier | come in | entrez |
| carpet | le tapis | company (firm) | la compagnie |
| carries, he | porte, il | contract | le contrat |
| carries, she | porte, elle | cook | le chef |
| carry, I | porte, je | cooker | le réchaud |
| carry, we | portons, nous | cool | frais |
| | | cool (f) | fraîche (f) |
| cash till | la caisse | cork | le bouchon |
| casino | le casino | corner | le coin |
| castle | le château | corridor | le couloir |

| | | | |
|---|---|---|---|
| cotton | le coton | distant (f) | lointaine (f) |
| countryside | la campagne | ditch | le fossé |
| cousin (f) | la cousine | do you speak | parlez-vous |
| cousin (m) | le cousin | English? | anglais? |
| cow | la vache | doctor | le médecin |
| crossroads | le carrefour | dog | le chien |
| crowd | la foule | door | la porte |
| cup | la tasse | doorbell | la sonnette |
| cupboard | le placard | dress | la robe |
| curtain | le rideau | drill | la perceuse |
| customs | la douane | drink | la boisson |
| cut (the) | la coupure | driver | le chauffeur |
| cutlery | le couvert | dry | sec |
| cylinder | le cylindre | dry (f) | sèche (f) |
| dance, I | danse, je | duck | le canard |
| dance, they (f) | dansent, elles | during | pendant |
| | | each (every) | chaque |
| dance, they (m) | dansent, ils | ear | l'oreille (f) |
| dance, we | dansons, nous | east | l'est (m) |
| | | Easter | Pâques (f.pl) |
| dance, you (formal or pl) | dansez, vous | easy | facile |
| | | eat, they (m) | mangent, ils |
| dance, you (informal) | danses, tu | eat, they (f) | mangent, elles |
| danger | le danger | eat, I | mange, je |
| dark (hair/skin f) | brune (f) | eat, to | manger |
| | | eat, you | mangez, vous |
| dark (hair/skin) | brun | | |
| daughter | la fille | eaten | mangé |
| day | le jour | eats | mange |
| December | décembre | egg | l'oeuf (m) |
| deep | profond | eight | huit |
| deep (f) | profonde (f) | electrician | l'électricien (m) |
| deer | le cerf | | |
| delicious | délicieux | electricity | l'électricité (f) |
| delicious (f) | délicieuse (f) | elephant | l'éléphant (m) |
| dentist | le dentiste | elegant | élégant |
| detour | la déviation | elegant (f) | élégante (f) |
| diet | le régime | eleven | onze |
| different | différent | empty | vide |
| different (f) | différente (f) | end | la fin |
| difficult | difficile | endless | éternel |
| dinghy | le canot | energetic | énergique |
| dinner | le diner | engaged | occupé |
| dirty | sale | English | anglais |
| distant | lointain | entrance | l'entrée (f) |

314

| everything | tout | full | plein |
| exhibition | l'exposition (f) | full (f) | pleine (f) |
| exit | la sortie | gangway | la passerelle |
| expensive | cher | garage | le garage |
| face | le visage | garden | le jardin |
| factory | l'usine (f) | gardener | le jardinier |
| false | faux | garlic | l'aïl (m) |
| false (f) | fausse | gasket | le joint |
| family | la famille | gate | la barrière |
| farmer | le fermier | geography | la géographie |
| father | le père | German | allemand |
| February | février | gift | le cadeau |
| field | le champ | girl | la jeune fille |
| fifth | cinquième | glass | le verre |
| fill, I | remplis, je | go, I | vais, je |
| find, I | trouve, je | goat | la chèvre |
| fire!!! | au feu! | gold(en) | doré |
| fireman | le pompier | good | bon |
| firm (solid) | ferme | good (f) | bonne (f) |
| first (f) | première | good evening | bonsoir |
| first (m) | premier | good luck | bonne chance |
| fish | le poisson | goodbye | au revoir |
| five | cinq | goods | la marchandise |
| flat (level) | plat | goose | l'oie (f) |
| flat (level) (f) | plate (f) | grandfather | le grand'père |
| flat (living) | l'appartement (m) | grandmother | la grand'mère |
| | | grandson | le petit-fils |
| flight | le vol | grass | l'herbe (f) |
| flood | le déluge | green | vert |
| floor | le plancher | green (f) | verte (f) |
| flower | la fleur | grey | gris |
| fly | la mouche | grey (f) | grise (f) |
| food | la nourriture | guest | l'invité (m or f) |
| forbidden | interdit | guide | le guide |
| forbidden (f) | interdite (f) | hail | la grêle |
| forest | la forêt | half | demi or |
| fork | lá fourchette | | demie (f) |
| fountain | la fontaine | hammer | le marteau |
| four | quatre | hand | la main |
| French | français | handkerchief | le mouchoir |
| French bread | la baguette | happy | heureux |
| fresh | frais | happy (f) | heureuse (f) |
| fresh (f) | fraîche | hard | dur |
| Friday | vendredi | has | a |
| frost | la gelée | hat | le chapeau |
| fruit | le fruit | hate, I | hais, je |

315

| | | | |
|---|---|---|---|
| have (they) | ont | how are you? | comment allez-vous? |
| have a good journey | bon voyage | how far is it? | c'est à quelle distance? |
| have, I | ai, j' | human being | l'être humain (m) |
| have, you | avez, vous | husband | le mari |
| he | il | I | je |
| healthy | sain | I don't know | je ne sais pas |
| healthy (f) | saine (f) | I don't understand | je ne comprends pas |
| hear, I | entends, j' | | |
| heavily | lourdement | | |
| heavy | lourd | ice | la glace |
| heavy (f) | lourde (f) | illness | la maladie |
| hedge | la haie | immediately | immediatement |
| hedgehog | le hérisson | | |
| heel | le talon | impossible | impossible |
| hello | bonjour | in | dans |
| help | au secours | in (+ month) | en |
| help, I | aide, j' | ink | l'encre (f) |
| hen | la poule | inn | l'auberge (f) |
| her | la (or l' + vowel) | insect | l'insecte (m) |
| her (f) | sa (f) | intelligent | intelligent |
| her (m) | son (m) | intelligent (+ f) | intelligente (f) |
| her (pl) | ses | | |
| her, to | lui | iron | le fer |
| here | ici | is | est |
| here is | voici | is there | y a-t-il |
| high | haut | island | l'île (f) |
| high (f) | haute (f) | it (f) | la (f) |
| him, to | lui | it (m) | le (m) |
| hire, I | loue, je | it, to | lui |
| his, (f) | sa (f) | Italian | italien |
| his (m) | son (m) | its (+ f) | sa (f) |
| his (pl) | ses | its (+ m) | son (m) |
| history | l'histoire (f) | jack | le cric |
| hole | le trou | jacket | la veste |
| holidays | les vacances (f) | January | janvier |
| horn | le klaxon | jewel | le bijou |
| horse | le cheval | journey | le voyage |
| hospital | l'hôpital (m) | July | juillet |
| hot | chaud | June | juin |
| hot (f) | chaude (f) | just a minute | une minute |
| hotel | l'hôtel (m) | kiss, I | embrasse, j' |
| hour | l'heure (f) | kitchen | la cuisine |
| house | la maison | knee | le genou |
| how | comment | | |

| | | | |
|---|---|---|---|
| knife | le couteau | midday | midi |
| ladder | l'échelle (f) | middle | le centre |
| landing | l'atterrissage (m) | midnight | minuit |
| | | milk | le lait |
| lawn | la pelouse | minus | moins |
| lazy | paresseux | minute | la minute |
| lazy (f) | paresseuse (f) | mistake | l'erreur (f) |
| leaf | la feuille | Monday | lundi |
| leather | le cuir | money | l'argent (m) |
| left | la gauche | money | |
| leg | la jambe | exchange | le change |
| less | moins | month | le mois |
| letter | la lettre | moon | la lune |
| lettuce | la salade | more | plus |
| lifebelt | la ceinture de sauvetage | morning | le matin |
| | | mother | la mère |
| lift | l'ascenseur (m) | motorway | l'autoroute (f) |
| light (weight) | léger | mountain | la montagne |
| light (weight) (f) | légère (f) | mouse | la souris |
| | | mouth | la bouche |
| lightning | l'éclair (m) | mushroom | le champignon |
| like, I | aime, j' | my (f) | ma (f) |
| lip | la lèvre | my (m) | mon (m) |
| liver, I (where) | habite, j' | my (pl) | mes (pl) |
| lobster | le homard | nail | le clou |
| lock | la serrure | nappy | la couche |
| lose, I | perds, je | narrow | étroit |
| lukewarm | tiède | narrow (f) | étroite (f) |
| lunch | le déjeuner | nephew | le neveu |
| mad | fou | new | nouveau |
| mad (f) | folle (f) | new (f) | nouvelle (f) |
| main | principal | newspaper | le journal |
| manager | le directeur | next | prochain |
| many | beaucoup (de) | next (f) | prochaine (f) |
| | | niece | la nièce |
| March | mars | night | la nuit |
| market | le marché | nine | neuf |
| maths | les mathémat-iques (f.pl) | no | non |
| | | north | le nord |
| | | not | ne . . . pas |
| May | mai | November | novembre |
| may I have? | pourrais-je avoir? | nurse | l'infirmière (f) |
| | | nut | l'écrou (m) |
| me | me | nylon | le nylon |
| meat | la viande | oar | la rame |
| menu | la carte | obvious | évident |

| | | | |
|---|---|---|---|
| obvious (f) | évidente (f) | physics | la physique |
| October | octobre | piano | le piano |
| of | de | picnic | le pique-nique |
| of the (+ vowel) | de l' | pink | rose |
| of the (f) | de la | pipe (to smoke) | la pipe |
| of the (m) | du | plate | l'assiette (f) |
| of the (pl) | des | platform | le quai |
| office | le bureau | please | s'il vous |
| oil | l'huile (f) | | plaît |
| on | sur | plumber | le plombier |
| on (days of the | | pocket | la poche |
| week) | le | police | la police |
| one | un | poor | pauvre |
| one (f) | une (f) | popular | populaire |
| open | ouvert | possible | possible |
| open (f) | ouverte (f) | postage stamp | le timbre |
| or | ou | potato | la pomme de |
| orange | orange | | terre |
| orchard | le verger | practical | pratique |
| our | notre | pretty | joli |
| our (pl) | nos | price | le prix |
| outskirts (of | | pullover | le pullover |
| town) | le faubourg | put, I | mets, je |
| oyster | l'huitre (f) | quarter | le quart |
| pain | la douleur | quay | le quai |
| pale | pâle | queue | la queue |
| pancake | la crêpe | quick | rapide |
| paper | le papier | quickly | rapidement |
| parcel | le colis | quiet | tranquille |
| parents | les parents | quiet | calme |
| | (m.pl) | quite | assez |
| passenger | le passager | rabbit | le lapin |
| passport | le passeport | radio | la radio |
| peach | le pêche | railway | le chemin |
| pear | la poire | | de fer |
| pebble | le galet | rain | la pluie |
| pedestrian | le piéton | rake | le râteau |
| pedestrian | le passage à | read, I | lis, je |
| crossing | piétons | read, to | lire |
| pen | le stylo | ready | prêt |
| pencil | le crayon | ready (f) | prête (f) |
| people | les gens | receipt | le reçu |
| perfect | parfait | recipe | la recette |
| perfect (f) | parfaite (f) | red | rouge |
| petal | le pétale | region | la région |
| petrol | l'essence (f) | relation (f) | la parente |

318

| | | | |
|---|---|---|---|
| relation (m) | le parent | see, I | vois, je |
| rent | le loyer | see, to | voir |
| restaurant | le restaurant | see, you | voyez, vous |
| rib | la côte | sees | voit |
| rice | le riz | sell, I | vends, je |
| rich | riche | September | septembre |
| right | la droite | serious (illness) | grave |
| ring | la bague | serious (not | |
| ripe | mûr | funny) | sérieux |
| ripe (f) | mûre (f) | serious (not | |
| river | la rivière | funny f) | sérieuse (f) |
| road | la route | serve, I | sers, je |
| roof | le toit | seven | sept |
| room | la pièce | she | elle |
| rope | la corde | sheep | le mouton |
| round | rond | sheet | le drap |
| round (f) | ronde (f) | shoe | la chaussure |
| roundabout | le rond-point | shop | le magasin |
| run, I | cours, je | short | court |
| sail | la voile | short (f) | courte (f) |
| sailor | le marin | show, I | montre, je |
| salary | le salaire | shrub | l'arbuste (m) |
| salesman | le vendeur | silencer | le silencieux |
| salt | le sel | silk | la soie |
| sand | le sable | sincere | sincère |
| sandwich | le sandwich | sister | la soeur |
| satisfied | satisfait | sitting, I am | assis, je suis |
| satisfied (f) | satisfaite (f) | six | six |
| Saturday | samedi | skin | la peau |
| sauce | la sauce | skirt | la jupe |
| saucepan | la casserole | sky | le ciel |
| say, I | dis, je | sleep, I | dors, je |
| scissors | les ciseaux | sleep, to | dormir |
| | (m.pl) | sleeve | la manche |
| scream, I | crie, je | slow | lent |
| screw | la vis | slow (f) | lente (f) |
| screwdriver | le tournevis | small | petit |
| sea | la mer | small (f) | petite (f) |
| seagull | la mouette | smoke, I | fume, je |
| seat | le siège | smooth | lisse |
| second | la seconde | snail | l'escargot (m) |
| secretary | la secrétaire | snow | la neige |
| see (they) | voient | soap | le savon |
| see you soon | à bientôt | sock | la chaussette |
| see you | | son | le fils |
| tommorow | à demain | soon | bientôt |

| | | | |
|---|---|---|---|
| south | le sud | ten | dix |
| souvenir | le souvenir | tent | la tente |
| spade | la bêche | than | que |
| Spanish | espagnol | thank you | merci |
| spanner | la clef | thanks for your | merci du |
| spark plug | la bougie | trouble | dérangement |
| speak slowly | parlez lentement | that's all | c'est tout |
| | | that's fine | c'est parfait |
| speak, I | parle, je | the (before vowel) | l' |
| speak, to | parler | the (fem. sing.) | la |
| special | spécial | the (masc. sing) | le |
| spoken | parlé | the (plural) | les |
| spoon | la cuiller | theatre | le théâtre |
| spring | le printemps | their | leur |
| stadium | le stade | them | les |
| stain | la tache | there | là |
| staircase | l'escalier (m) | these/those (pl) | ces |
| star | l'étoile (f) | they (f) | elles |
| station | la gare | they (m) | ils |
| steel | l'acier (m) | thief | le voleur |
| stick | le bâton | thigh | la cuisse |
| stone | la pierre | thin | mince |
| straight | droit | third | troisième |
| straight (f) | droite (f) | this way | par ici |
| strange | bizarre | this/that (f) | cette |
| street | la rue | this/that (m) | ce |
| striker | le gréviste | three | trois |
| strong | fort | throat | la gorge |
| strong (f) | forte (f) | thumb | le pouce |
| stupid | stupide | thunder | le tonnerre |
| sugar | le sucre | Thursday | jeudi |
| suitable | convenable | ticket | le billet |
| suitcase | la valise | tide | la marée |
| summer | l'été (m) | time | le temps |
| sun | le soleil | tip | le pourboire |
| Sunday | dimanche | tired | fatigué |
| sure | sûr | tired (f) | fatiguée (f) |
| sure (f) | sûre (f) | to | à |
| table | la table | to the (f) | à la |
| tablecloth | la nappe | to the (m) | au |
| take-off | l'envol (m) | toast | le pain grillé |
| tap | le robinet | toilet | les toilettes (f.pl) |
| telephone | le téléphone | | |
| television | la télévision | toll | le péage |
| temple (medical) | la tempe | tomato | la tomate |

| | | | |
|---|---|---|---|
| tongue | la langue | wall | le mur |
| torch | la lampe | want (they) | veulent |
| tourist | le touriste | want, I | veux, je |
| towel | la serviette | want, you | voulez, vous |
| town | la ville | wants | veut |
| town hall | la mairie | wardrobe | l'armoire (f) |
| town square | la place | was | était |
| traffic (road) | la circulation | wasp | la guêpe |
| tree | l'arbre (m) | water | l'eau (f) |
| trousers | le pantalon | we | nous |
| trout | la truite | weak | faible |
| true | vrai | weather | le temps |
| Tuesday | mardi | Wednesday | mercredi |
| twenty-five | vingt-cinq | weed | la mauvaise |
| two | deux | | herbe |
| tyre | le pneu | week | a semaine |
| ugly | laid | well behaved | sage |
| ugly (f) | laide (f) | were | étaient |
| uncle | l'oncle (m) | west | l'ouest (m) |
| under | sous | wet | mouillé |
| underground | | wet (f) | mouillée |
| (the) | le metro | what time is it? | quelle heure |
| underpants | le slip | | est il? |
| understand, I | comprends, | what's the | qu'est-ce |
| | je | matter? | qu'il y a? |
| unhappy | malheureux | what? | quelle? |
| unhappy (f) | malheureuse | wheel barrow | la brouette |
| | (f) | when | quand |
| urgent | urgent | where | où |
| urgent (f) | urgente (f) | where are . . .? | où sont? |
| us | nous | where is . . .? | où est? |
| valve | la soupape | white | blanc |
| veal | le veau | white (f) | blanche (f) |
| vegetable | le légume | why | pourquoi |
| vein | la veine | wide | large |
| velvet | le velours | widow | la veuve |
| very | trés | widower | le veuf |
| very well | très bien | wife | la femme |
| villa | la villa | wind | le vent |
| vinegar | le vinaigre | window | la fenêtre |
| violent | violent | windscreen | l'essuie-gace |
| violent (f) | violente (f) | wiper | (m) |
| vulgar | vulgaire | wine | le vin |
| waiter | le garçon | winter | l'hiver (m) |
| waitress | la serveuse | wire | le fil |
| walk, a | la promenade | with | avec |

| | | | |
|---|---|---|---|
| without | sans | year | l'an (m) |
| wonderful | merveilleux | yellow | jaune |
| wonderful (f) | merveilleuse (f) | yes | oui |
| wool | la laine | you (formal + pl) | vous |
| worker | l'ouvrier (m) | you (informal) | tu |
| worried | inquiet | young | jeune |
| worried (f) | inquiete (f) | your | votre |
| worse or worst | pire | your (pl) | vos |
| write, I | écris, j' | zero | zéro |
| written | écrit | | |

# LINKWORD LANGUAGE SYSTEM

**The fastest, the easiest, the most enjoyable way to learn a language!**

Pick up 400 words and basic grammar in just 12 hours with LINKWORD

\* Travelling \* Eating Out \* Telling the Time \* Emergencies
\* At the Hotel \* Going Shopping \* Numbers \* Clothes
\* Family \* On the Beach

**Ideal for holidays, business travel, schoolwork**

'Unforgettable memory joggers'
*The Sunday Times*

'It took 12 hours to teach a regime that normally takes 40 hours'
*Training manager, Thomson Holidays*

'It works and it's fun'
*Guardian*

Available for the following languages

| | |
|---|---|
| 0 552 130532 **FRENCH** | 0 552 130540 **GERMAN** |
| 0 552 130559 **SPANISH** | 0 552 130567 **ITALIAN** |
| 0 552 139068 **PORTUGUESE** | 0 552 139076 **GREEK** |

# LINKWORD AUDIO TAPES

An audio tape is available as an extra learning aid to accompany this book.

It allows you to hear and to practise the correct pronunciation for all the words used on this course.

The tape is available by mail order using the order form at the back of this book.

Other LINKWORD AUDIO TAPES:

0 552 13225X  French
0 552 132268  German
0 552 132276  Spanish
0 552 132284  Italian
0 552 139661  Portuguese
0 552 139556  Greek
0 552 140317  Further French

## LINKWORD BOOK AND AUDIO TAPE PACKS

The following LINKWORD courses are also available in packs combining the books with the relevant pronunciation cassette tape.

These are available either by mail order, using the form at the back of this book, or you can buy the pack from any good bookshop:

0 552 005002 French
0 552 005010 Spanish

## LINKWORD LANGUAGE SYSTEM BOOKS, AUDIO TAPES AND BOOK AND TAPE PACKS AVAILABLE FROM CORGI BOOKS

THE PRICES SHOWN BELOW WERE CORRECT AT THE TIME OF GOING TO PRESS. HOWEVER TRANSWORLD PUBLISHERS RESERVE THE RIGHT TO SHOW NEW RETAIL PRICES ON COVERS WHICH MAY DIFFER FROM THOSE PREVIOUSLY ADVERTISED IN THE TEXT OR ELSEWHERE.

| | | | |
|---|---|---|---|
| ☐ | 13053 2 | LINKWORD LANGUAGE SYSTEM: FRENCH | £4.99 |
| ☐ | 13054 0 | LINKWORD LANGUAGE SYSTEM: GERMAN | £4.99 |
| ☐ | 13055 9 | LINKWORD LANGUAGE SYSTEM: SPANISH | £4.99 |
| ☐ | 13056 7 | LINKWORD LANGUAGE SYSTEM: ITALIAN | £4.99 |
| ☐ | 13907 6 | LINKWORD LANGUAGE SYSTEM: GREEK | £4.99 |
| ☐ | 13906 8 | LINKWORD LANGUAGE SYSTEM: PORTUGUESE | £4.99 |
| ☐ | 13225 X | LINKWORD AUDIO TAPE: FRENCH | £6.95 |
| ☐ | 14031 7 | LINKWORD AUDIO TAPE: FURTHER FRENCH | £6.95 |
| ☐ | 13226 8 | LINKWORD AUDIO TAPE: GERMAN | £6.95 |
| ☐ | 13227 6 | LINKWORD AUDIO TAPE: SPANISH | £6.95 |
| ☐ | 13228 4 | LINKWORD AUDIO TAPE: ITALIAN | £6.95 |
| ☐ | 13955 6 | LINKWORD AUDIO TAPE: GREEK | £6.95 |
| ☐ | 13966 1 | LINKWORD AUDIO TAPE: PORTUGUESE | £6.95 |
| ☐ | 13957 2 | LINKWORD BOOK AND TAPE PACK: FRENCH | £9.99 |
| ☐ | 13959 9 | LINKWORD BOOK AND TAPE PACK: SPANISH | £9.99 |

All Corgi/Bantam Books are available at your bookshop or newsagent, or can be ordered from the following address:

Corgi/Bantam Books,
Cash Sales Department
P.O. Box 11, Falmouth, Cornwall TR10 9EN

UK and B.F.P.O. customers please send a cheque or postal order (no currency) and allow £1.00 for postage and packing for the first book plus 50p for the second book and 30p for each additional book to a maximum charge of £3.00 (7 books plus).

Overseas customers, including Eire, please allow £2.00 for postage and packing for the first book plus £1.00 for the second book and 50p for each subsequent title ordered.

NAME (Block Letters) ........................................................................................................................

ADDRESS ........................................................................................................................

........................................................................................................................